T0094390

Narrative Tactics for Mobile and Social Games

Pocket-Sized Storytelling

Narrative Tactics for Mobile and Social Games

Pocket-Sized Storytelling

Edited by
Toiya Kristen Finley, PhD

CRC Press
Taylor & Francis Group
Boca Raton London New York

CRC Press is an imprint of the
Taylor & Francis Group, an **informa** business

CRC Press
Taylor & Francis Group
6000 Broken Sound Parkway NW, Suite 300
Boca Raton, FL 33487-2742

© 2019 by Taylor & Francis Group, LLC
CRC Press is an imprint of Taylor & Francis Group, an Informa business

No claim to original U.S. Government works

Printed on acid-free paper

International Standard Book Number-13: 978-1-4987-8078-0 (paperback)
International Standard Book Number-13: 978-1-1386-1393-5 (hardback)

Library of Congress Cataloging-in-Publication Data

Names: Finley, Toiya Kristen, editor.
Title: Narrative tactics for mobile and social games : pocket-sized storytelling / [edited by] Toiya Kristen Finley.
Description: Boca Raton : Taylor & Francis, CRC Press, 2018. | Includes bibliographical references.
Identifiers: LCCN 2018010535| ISBN 9781498780780 (pbk. : alk. paper) | ISBN 9781138613935 (hardback : alk. paper)
Subjects: LCSH: Narration (Rhetoric) | Rhetoric and psychology. | Video games-- Psychological aspects.
Classification: LCC PE1425 .N38 2018 | DDC 808/.036--dc23
LC record available at https://lccn.loc.gov/2018010535

Visit the Taylor & Francis Web site at
http://www.taylorandfrancis.com

and the CRC Press Web site at
http://www.crcpress.com

contents

Section I
storytelling in mobile and social games

acknowledgements

I would like to thank all of the developers and companies who gave permission to *Narrative Tactics in Mobile and Social Games*'s contributors to use screenshots in their chapters. Being able to look at visuals next to our analysis is extremely beneficial to our readers. I'm especially grateful to Kenji-san of IGDA Japan and Allan Simonsen for getting me in touch with contacts.

To Myra Finley (publication's on your birthday!) and Lakeview, thanks for your continued support, even if you're not quite sure what the heck it is that I do. :)

To Sean Connelly, I'm grateful to you for greenlighting the project. To Alex Kain and Richard Dansky, thanks for your support during the initial stages and your vote of confidence. To Jessica Vega, thanks for your hard work in keeping everything on track and on schedule.

To Heather Albano and Rachel Ginsberg, thanks for being awesome beta readers and providing your expertise and great feedback. Meghan Connor, your graphics help at the last minute was project-saving!

And special thanks to this book's contributors—Betsy, Elizabeth, Jessica, Megan, Eddy, and Erin—for sharing your insights with the rest of us.

contributors

Betsy Brey is a PhD candidate specializing in game studies at the University of Waterloo's Department of English Language and Literature. Her research focuses on the narratological impacts of game mechanics, how game stories are created throughout gameplay processes. In particular, she researches mechanics and storytelling in roleplaying games. She works with the University of Waterloo's Games Institute, where her research has been funded with a Mitacs partnership. She is also the editor-in-chief for *First Person Scholar*, an open-access, multidisciplinary game studies publication.

Megan Fausti is the narrative designer for *Battle Chef Brigade* and an advocate for weirder, more compassionate games at Adult Swim Games (ASG). During her time at ASG, she's worked on everything it has published since *Oblitus*, for a total of more than 30 shipped games across PC, VR, console, and mobile. In her free time she loves videogames, matcha lattes, and nature documentaries.

Toiya Kristen Finley, PhD, a Nashville native, is a writer and an editor. She holds a doctorate in literature and creative writing from Binghamton University. With nearly 70 published works in fiction, nonfiction, comics/manga, and games, she has 20 years of experience writing in a range of genres, tones, styles, and voices. In 2011, she cofounded the Game Writing Tutorial at GDC Online with Tobias Heussner and served as an instructor in 2011 and 2012. In videogames, she has worked as a game designer, narrative designer, game writer, and editor (or some combination of the four) on several unreleased and in-production indie, social, and mobile games for children and general audiences. Several of these projects' existences shall remain forever a secret (hey, that's the game industry for ya). Some published games include *Academagia: The Making of Mages* (Black Chicken Studios), *Fat Chicken* (Relevant Games), *Peregrin* (Domino Digital Limited), and *Verdant Skies* (Howling Moon Software). She is currently a member of the IGDA Game Writing Special Interest Group's Executive Board and teaches game writing and narrative design for the UCLA Extension Writers' Program. She coauthored *The Game Narrative Toolbox* (Focal Press, 2015), a book on narrative design, with Jennifer Brandes Hepler, Ann Lemay, and Tobias Heussner.

Erin Hoffman-John is the chief designer and CEO of Sense of Wonder, an independent mobile developer of "smart fun" games. Prior to these roles, she led game design at GlassLab, a three-year initiative to establish integrated formative assessment educational games, which was supported by the Bill and Melinda Gates Foundation and the Macarthur Foundation. Her game credits include *Mars Generation One: Argubot Academy*, *Kung Fu Panda World*, and *GoPets*. She is also the author of a fantasy trilogy with Pyr Books. For more information, visit http://www.makingwonder.com, http://www.glasslabgames.org, and @gryphoness on Twitter.

Elizabeth LaPensée, PhD, is an award-winning designer, writer, artist, and researcher of Indigenous-led media, such as games and comics. She is settler-Irish, Anishinaabe with relations from Bay Mills Indian Community and Michif. She is an Assistant Professor of Media & Information and Writing, Rhetoric & American Cultures at Michigan State University. She designed and created art for *Thunderbird Strike* (2017), a lightning-searing side-scroller game that won Best Digital Media at imagineNATIVE Film + Media Arts Festival. She was a writer for *Where the Water Tastes Like Wine* (Dim Bulb Games and Serenity Forge/Good Shepherd Entertainment, 2017), awarded Developers Choice at IndieCade.

Jessica Sliwinski has more than a decade of experience in the videogame industry, having written for everything from AAA MMOs to indie mobile games. After four years writing quest content for BioWare's *Star Wars: The Old Republic* and its first expansion, *Rise of the Hutt Cartel*, she got a crash course in mobile game design at Zynga, writing for *The Ville*. Now in her sixth year as lead narrative designer for Disruptor Beam, Jessica uses lessons learned from creating both expansive cinematic experiences and single-string quest intros to inform narrative design for story-driven mobile games, such as *The Walking Dead: March to War*, *Star Trek Timelines*, and *Game of Thrones Ascent*.

Eddy Webb (with a "y," thank you) is a writer, design consultant, and game and narrative designer for videogames and RPGs. He's worked on over a hundred books and games during his career. He has created unique game universes, such as the world of Pugmire. He's also partnered with companies to work on established properties like *Futurama*, *Firefly*, *Red Dwarf*, the WWE, and Sherlock Holmes. He's even won a few awards over the past decade or so. In his spare time, he advocates for more inclusion of people with hearing loss. He can be found at pugsteady.com and eddyfate.com.

introduction

an untold story

Narrative designers and writers are using some clever concepts to mature storytelling in mobile and social games. Back in their early days on Facebook and Google Plus, social games weren't known for in-depth story. And because of early smartphone technology, mobile games were a lot simpler. However, I would argue that mobile and social games have fostered some of the most innovative storytelling techniques today, partly because of their restrictions. Mobile developers have to make sure that their games work on tablets and phones, for a variety of models with different technological limitations. Smaller storage capacities mean developers have fewer sound, animation, and art assets to incorporate into their storytelling.

Mobile and social games create other storytelling limitations developers must take into account—player habits and expectations. The Entertainment Software Association learned in 2015 that commuters spend a third of their time playing games on their phone.[*] With the average play session clocking in at 7.5 minutes,[†] the *way* mobile games deliver stories has to be a little different from traditional

---

[*] Entertainment Software Association, "Commuters spend nearly one-third of travel time playing games," *TheESA.com*, last modified August 12, 2015, http://www.theesa .com/article/commuters-spend-nearly-one-third-of-travel-time-playing-games/.

[†] Yaniv Nizan, "33 mobile game benchmarks and rules of thumb," *Sooma Blog*, last modified August 14, 2016, http://blog.soom.la/2016/08/33-benchmarks-in-mobile -games-business.html.

videogames. If your stop's approaching, and you need to hop off the bus, you probably don't want to sit through a long cutscene. And, as it's true with console and PC games, there are players who just don't care about story and want to skip all the story bits. Therefore, in mobile games, we need techniques to communicate the important parts of the story without making players feel we're interrupting or slowing down what they most enjoy about the game.

Mobile games now make more money than console and PC games.* A range of demographics worldwide play them, including people who never cared about games before they got their first smartphone.† The mobile space is fiercely competitive. With so many games for players to choose from, why not give yours great storytelling to help it stand out? Attention to the game's narrative design and story increases its production values and can be one more thing that gets players to consider installing or purchasing it.

I wrote content on mobile and social games for *The Game Narrative Toolbox* (coauthored with Jennifer Brandes Hepler, Ann Lemay, and Tobias Heussner). This book continues that discussion and devotes its chapters specifically to issues mobile and social games address when it comes to their narrative design and game writing. Joining me are contributors Betsy Brey and Elizabeth LaPensée, PhD, Jessica Sliwinski, Megan Fausti, Eddy Webb, Erin Hoffman-John, and Carl Varnado.‡

Narrative Tactics for Mobile and Social Games: Pocket-Sized Storytelling has two parts. Section I: Storytelling in Mobile and Social Games covers aspects of storytelling, such as worldbuilding, dialogue, and quests, and looks at facilitating player agency and telling stories in games that aren't story oriented. Section II: Storytelling for Different Demographics and Genres looks at types of mobile and social games and their audiences.

---

* Stephanie Chan, "Mobile game revenue finally surpasses PC and consoles," last modified July 13, 2017, https://venturebeat.com/2017/07/13/mobile-game-revenue -finally-surpasses-pc-and-consoles/.
† My septuagenarian aunt among them.
‡ Please see Carl's essay on transmedia mobile games on *Narrative Tactics for Mobile and Social Games's* website: https://www.crcpress.com/Narrative-Tactics-for-Mobile -and-Social-Games-Pocket-Sized-Storytelling/Finley/p/book/9781498780780. (Forthcoming.)

Over the past several years, the industry is focusing more and more on how to include great narrative in games. It's time the fantastic work mobile developers are doing on their stories becomes part of that conversation. I hope this book gives you ideas for your project, whether you consider yourself to be a writer or not. And, just maybe, we can pick up a few innovations for traditional videogames too.

Toiya Kristen Finley, PhD

I

storytelling in mobile and social games

keeping the player at the heart of the story

Toiya Kristen Finley, PhD

contents

Here's a premise for you:

> *It's you against the world...*
>
> *A fight for survival, you have to wipe out all of your enemies, or they'll obliterate you from existence. You must do whatever you can to stay alive. Outwit them before they figure out your plans. If you want to defeat them—all of humanity—you're going to have to do destructive things, horrible things.*
>
> *But you'll get to live as a conqueror if you do.*

Would you consider the above premise story oriented? (We'll get back to this a little later.)

Get into a discussion about what makes videogames special, and it's not long before someone brings up that they're an active medium, unlike prose fiction, comics/manga, film, animation, or TV. The game involves players who are involved in what happens. Through gameplay and controls, players change what's happening to the world. In a level, they may destroy every building on the map while hunting aliens. Or they may help all of the nonplayer characters (NPCs) in a town capture or kill a group of bandits. They can interact with certain NPCs and choose responses in dialogue trees. Other choices they make might alter the story's plot or characters' lives. Videogames, an active medium, feed player agency.*

In addition to player agency, many console, PC, and online games offer increasingly realistic levels of immersion. They place player characters (PCs)—and players, by extension—into a world where players can roam around and explore. Whether that world is rendered in 2D, isometric 3D, 3D, or VR, it has terrains to walk, run, or climb. Players can look at their screens and see NPCs interact with player characters. They might hear a "BOOM!" followed by shouting

---

* Player agency is the sense that players have autonomy or control over their gameplay experience. Of course, they don't have complete control because they can only do what the code will allow. But everything that happens during their gaming sessions—whether they're successful, whether they fail, when they choose to tap the screen, how they move the thumbstick, the NPCs they choose to talk to or not talk to, whether they decide to fight a boss or stealthily get around it—these are the players' decisions, and they have meaningful outcomes.

behind them, alerting them to backtrack to see what the excitement's about. Through mechanics, sound, animation, art, and other assets, these traditional games* have multiple techniques that engage players and hook their interest.

Because of technological limitations and smaller storage capacities on smartphones and tablets, mobile and social games have historically been at a disadvantage when it comes to facilitating immersion and player agency. With the advancements in mobile devices, more and more mobile and social games have the characteristics of these worlds found in console, PC, and online games. However, many still can't render the complexity of the worlds we've become accustomed to in traditional videogames. They don't allow players to complete a mission based upon a certain play style (like stealth mode or no killing), which would in turn affect variable story and gameplay outcomes. They don't let players side with one character over another, unlocking a new branch in the story. And they don't have multiple endings. In effect, many of these games have linear stories the player doesn't influence at all.

These technological disadvantages of mobile games can lead to a storytelling consequence: players feel as if they're *watching* a story instead of *participating* in it. Players also complain that the typical mobile game does not integrate the story, world, and characters into its gameplay. Additionally, some of the techniques we use in traditional games, like the cutscene, may not be feasible in mobile. A lot of players dread cutscenes in traditional and mobile games because they take away from the action and gameplay—the parts of the game they care about the most. A cutscene in a mobile game may be even more frustrating because it cuts into the limited time players have for sessions while waiting in the doctor's office. Or they don't feel a part of the game's story because there's no avatar representing them in the game, and the PC is unseen. Even worse, developers don't take the game's narrative design into account at all.

But all of these are solvable problems. We can make mobile and social games player-centric even though we don't have the same technological advantages of traditional games.

I was working as a narrative designer with Relevant Games on a mobile game that was never released. Our story was interstitial between the gameplay segments and linear with no player choices.

---

* I'm using "traditional" to mean PC, console, and online games (MMOs, MMORPGs, and MOBAs).

We realized the unseen PC was passive and at the whims of the NPCs' decision-making. As we puzzled over fixing this problem, creative director Joshua Mills asked a provocative question, "How do we keep the player at the heart of the story?" Whether the game is story-oriented or not, there are tricks we can use that aid players in feeling like they're driving the action and/or plot.

There are a few things we need to keep in mind: (1) we can think of mobile and social games as a game *space*, (2) we need to remember that narrative design is just as essential in mobile and social games as it is in traditional games, and (3) *players' imaginations* are powerful tools that aid us in telling stories. We can use great narrative design to keep players engaged in the game space and use that game space to reflect every aspect of the story.

story delivery vs. story

We can use the game's space for its story delivery.

Storytelling goes beyond dialogue and cutscenes. Storytelling is more than words, and a game's narrative design can use any aspect of the game to contribute to its storytelling. A common way for explaining the concept of *narrative design* is "It serves as a bridge between gameplay and story." That's pretty good, but I don't think it's quite complete. Suggesting there needs to be a bridge between the two says that gameplay and story are *separate*.

I like to say that narrative design ensures that the story and world *embody* the gameplay. After all, gameplay and game design are types of storytelling, too. Players use all of the things they can do in a game to create their own narratives. (How many times have you heard a friend recount what they did during a playthrough, as if they were actually there, among the polygons? How many times have *you* done this?) The story and world can influence and inspire gameplay so that players can stay immersed and tell their own stories.

So, any part of the game players interact with is the game space, and any part of the game space can be a part of the game's narrative design.

Game writing, then, is what we think of as traditional storytelling:

- plot told through campaigns,
- plot told through missions and quests,

- dialogue, and
- cutscenes and cinematics.

Narrative design uses writing and other aspects of the game as storytelling vehicles. Depending on the game's needs, you may implement narrative design and writing, or only narrative design.

story delivery = narrative design

We can simplify game writing vs. narrative design even further and say that game writing = story, while narrative design = story delivery.

It's important to note that for some jobs, you may only work on the story part of the game. However, if you're working for smaller studios or clients who are new to game development (or the development team is only you), you may see yourself working on other areas of the game or informing your clients that they need to pay attention to these details.

In addition, narrative designers and game writers work closely with the entire team to implement the game's story. "A Game's Narrative Design" covers different aspects of narrative design and game writing and members of the development team who might be involved in implementing them.

A Game's Narrative Design

Narrative design encompasses the following.

Worldbuilding

These are the details that inform what the world is like and how you present that world to players. It includes

- the overarching history of the world,
- the timeline of events,
- cultures/societies,
- religions,
- magic/technology/science systems,
- languages,
- etc.

Everyone on the team is involved in worldbuilding. Players interact with the world (game space). Creative leads, producers, programmers, game designers, level designers, artists, animators, and sound designers work together to create the world.

We'll discuss worldbuilding more in Chapter 3, "Livable and Believable, Despite the Limitations: Worldbuilding."

Narrative structure

The narrative designer usually doesn't choose what type of structure the game will have at larger studios, but you may be a part of this decision-making with smaller clients, clients new to game development, or smaller studio teams.

Narrative structure can be

- linear (players don't help determine the story's plot/direction);
- branching (players make decisions that affect the story's plot, characters, and/or world);
- open (the story doesn't have a set structure, players "find" scenarios/quests with which to interact, and there are several alternative paths to get to the story's ending); and/or
- episodic (the game, and the story by extension, is released in installments).

Creative leads, producers, game designers, and game writers plan narrative structure with the narrative designer.

Character and creature design

Narrative design influences who and what inhabits the world/game space. Narrative designers work on

- character bios and histories,
- descriptions and "looks" of the character or creature,
- animation descriptions and suggestions for the character or creature,
- relationships characters have to each other and how these develop/ change, and
- story/mission arcs in which characters are involved.

Creative leads, producers, game designers, narrative designers, gamer writers, editors, artists, animators, and sound designers help shape characters and creatures. Voice directors may also be involved if the characters/creatures are voiced.

Environmental narrative

Environmental narrative is what the world tells players about itself. Environmental narrative communicates through

- interaction with objects,
- ambient dialogue,

- ambient sounds,
- haptic feedback,
- state change cues,
- etc.

Depending on the assets used for environmental narrative (like sound and animations), narrative designers will need to work with sound designers, animators, and artists. Creative leads, game designers, level designers, narrative designers, and game writers work to create a game's environmental narrative.

Location design

What places will the player visit and explore? The narrative designer thinks about

- what the location's function is in the world and what the inhabitants do there,
- how players interact with the location,
- what missions or quests are situated at the location, and
- what the location looks like.

Location design is a part of environmental narrative and includes the same team members as above.

Story integration into gameplay and mechanics

One of the most immersive tools narrative design has is using the gameplay and mechanics to inform the player about the world. Mechanics can do everything from reflecting PCs' personalities through their abilities to revealing hidden secrets about a place when players destroy obstacles. When thinking about story delivery through gameplay and mechanics, consider

- the mechanics themselves and what they might illustrate about the world or characters to the player, and
- the objects or features that players interact with via mechanics.

For more on this, please see the analysis on *Mystery Match* later in this chapter.

Working with the narrative designer, creative leads, producers, and game designers are integral to coming up with a plan for story integration into gameplay.

Overall tone

The game's narrative design must stay consistent throughout. Otherwise, it can be unbelievable, break player immersion, and work against player agency. Gritty horror writing would clash with surrealist art, for example. Psychedelic horror would be the much better fit.

The overall tone includes

- consistency of tone in all writing (dialogue, flavor text, instructions, etc.);
- the "look"/aesthetics of the game from art assets to UI and menus; and
- the sound of the game, including music.

The entire team is responsible for establishing and maintaining a consistent tone.

Dialogue delivery

If the game has dialogue, you'll need to think about how it's presented to the player:

- Does the game have branching dialogue? How complicated are the branches? What type of information or questions will you include in the conversation trees?
- Is the dialogue text based or voiced?
- What do the dialogue text boxes look like, and how do you position character portraits around them?
- How many lines, characters, and/or words do you include per dialogue text box?

Creative leads, producers, game designers, artists, UI designers, and narrative designers help design the look and placement of the text boxes, and game writers and/or narrative designers compose dialogue.

We'll look at dialogue in Chapter 5, "More Than Pretty Words: Functional Dialogue."

Cutscenes vs. animatics vs. neither

How do you deliver scenes for major plot points if your game has them?

- Are there any technical constraints when it comes to fully animated cutscenes or animatics?*
- Does the game need cutscenes or animatics?
- Can the game afford them? If not, what alternatives can you suggest?

---

* Cutscenes are in-engine, animated scenes that advance the plot and/or develop characters. Cutscenes can happen at any time, although they're usually placed before and after levels, stages, or quests/missions. Cutscenes can also be interactive. These allow player dialogue choices. Animatics are a way to present cutscenes using still images or comic book panels in sequence instead of animations. Like cutscenes, animatics can be voiced or text-based and include a soundtrack.

As is the case with dialogue, the same team members have a role in creating cutscenes and animatics. Animators, sound designers, and composers are also involved if the cutscenes are animated, involve sound effects for the text, and/or include music.

UI design

The look of the UI and menus can also say a lot about the world of the game and can keep players immersed in that world, even when they're not playing. The UI design must match the overall tone, aesthetic, and genre of the game. That may be obvious to us, but if your clients aren't game developers, this is something you can explain to them.

UI designers, creative leads, producers, game designers, and narrative designers all contribute to the look of the UI and menus.

Quest or mission design and structure

Quest/missions are important motivators to keep mobile players active. Here are some essential questions for story delivery:

- How do they fit into the main story?
- How long should they be?
- Are there side quests?
- Are there quest chains, and how many quests are in each chain?

Creative leads, producers, game designers, narrative designers, and game writers help with determining quests for the game and where they fall in story campaigns.

Read more about quest design in Chapter 6, "I Seek the Grail (in Five Minutes or Less): Designing and Writing Quests for Mobile Games."

Sound design

Players learn a lot about a world and its characters by what they hear. Some of the ways narrative design uses sound include

- sound effects,
- state changes, and
- music.

Along with sound designers, creative leads, producers, game designers, and narrative designers have a part in planning a game's sound assets. Additionally, if a game has music, you'll want to involve composers at or near the start of development. The composer will have more time to incorporate themes into the game's soundscape.

story delivery and the player's imagination

As writers, we've had the maxim "Show, don't tell," pounded into our brains. As game writers and narrative designers, we've learned "Play, don't tell." But we don't *need* to show players everything in a game, and they don't need to play (or experience) everything to make the narrative design believable. We can *suggest* and let the players' imaginations take over. Any and all story delivery techniques aid in engaging players' imaginations. The following mobile games are very different in genre and story, but they're effective at suggesting and making their narrative player centric.

Mystery Match (2015)

Emma Fairfax is *Mystery Match's* (Outplay Entertainment) fixed character.* Because of her bloodline, she is one of only a few people in the world who can operate peculiar (and sometimes diabolical) puzzle boxes. Emma runs a detective agency with her partner Julian Beaumont, and the two uncover a secret society's centuries-old conspiracy. Traveling the world, they encounter several NPCs who turn out to be both friend and foe.

Players don't get to make any decisions for Emma in this linear story. They don't get to choose whether they'll trust characters or what Emma will say to them. However, the game has a clever way of getting the player to identify with Emma. At the very beginning, the game shows players how to move gems around the puzzle boxes. Emma's animated index finger appears on the screen, guiding players as to which direction they need to swipe. Players literally touch and move gems on the screen with their fingers, just as Emma does. Using smartphones' and tablets' touchscreens is a huge advantage mobile games have over traditional games. Unlike controllers and keyboards, touchscreens provide a level of interaction and emotional engagement through direct contact with the game. In tutorials, *Mystery Match* delivers story via its mechanics to connect Emma to the player. The player, in fact, *is* Emma.

---

* Unlike customizable characters or customizable characters with fixed backgrounds, players can't determine the backstory, personality, or appearance of fixed characters.

As the game introduces new puzzle mechanics, Emma and Julian analyze the puzzle box and quickly assess what to do. The player sees Emma's index finger and then mimics its movement. It's important for the player to see this once in a while. It reconnects the player to Emma every so often as the story progresses.

Each puzzle box is a level. After the player completes several levels, the story progresses. In addition, some puzzle boxes reveal important clues to Emma's past and the conspiracy. Some puzzle boxes are weapons spewing dangerous poison, and Emma has to solve them to keep the danger from spreading.

Screenshot from *Mystery Match*. Developed/published by Outplay Entertainment and protected by United States and international copyright law. © Outplay Entertainment

Also of note—the all-important "SKIP" button at the top right of the screen. Screenshot from *Mystery Match*. Developed/published by Outplay Entertainment and protected by United States and international copyright law. © Outplay Entertainment

When the player completes a level, Emma solves a puzzle box. Emma's victories are the player's victories. Her heroism belongs to the player. Through the game's mechanics, the player feels in control of the story and Emma's successes. Emma (the player) advances the story only by completing puzzles.

You might want to include cutscenes, but you have budget or technical limitations. There are ways to get around those issues, too. *Mystery Match* has cutscenes using character portraits and text boxes. Each character in the game has a few portraits with different poses and expressions. Those poses and expressions change based upon the characters' emotional states and what's happening in the story. So, cutscenes are created by switching between these portraits and giving dialogue in text boxes.

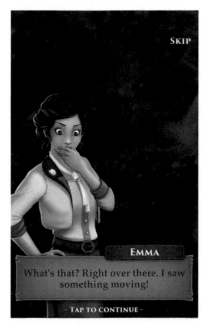

Screenshot from *Mystery Match*. Developed/published by Outplay Entertainment and protected by United States and international copyright law. © Outplay Entertainment

Screenshot from *Mystery Match*. Developed/published by Outplay Entertainment and protected by United States and international copyright law. © Outplay Entertainment

Screenshot from *Mystery Match*. Developed/published by Outplay Entertainment and protected by United States and international copyright law. © Outplay Entertainment

Screenshots taken from an earlier version of the game. Screenshot from *Mystery Match*. Developed/published by Outplay Entertainment and protected by Unted States and international copyright law. © Outplay Entertainment

Notice that they're talking about a jaguar. In this part of the story, Emma and Julian are exploring Mayan ruins, but we don't have any backgrounds to suggest that. The dialogue is enough to let us know where they are.

Plague Inc. (2012)

As I mentioned earlier, one thing to keep in mind is that players' imaginations are powerful storytelling tools. Games are successful whether they have photorealistic or retro graphics. They're successful experiences when their stories are 80 hours long, and there are lots of NPCs to interact with, or the game takes less than half an hour to play, and there's nothing but text on the screen.

We don't have to show or tell players everything for them to find the narrative enjoyable.

In fact, a game can make as powerful (or even *more* powerful) an impact on players if they fill in the unseen with their own imaginations. Instead of us telling them what's funny, scary, or heartbreaking, they can picture or hear what is the most impactful from *their* perspectives.

Remember that story premise I shared with you at the beginning of this chapter? That's based on the conflict in *Plague Inc.* (Ndemic Creations), a game decidedly not story focused. *Plague Inc.* states absolutely nothing from that premise anywhere in the game. However, based on the gameplay, it's easy for me to come up with that scenario as I play. The game itself is part strategy and part simulation. Players take the role of a disease (bacteria, virus, bioagent, etc.) that slowly infects the world, evolves, and grows more and more virulent. As the nations of the world learn of the disease, they shut down seaports and airports, kill off animals that may carry the disease, hand out bottled water instead of letting their citizens drink diseased water, and burn infected corpses. They work together to develop cures and eradicate the disease.

The main screen engaging players is a map of the world where they see how the disease spreads, how quickly country populations die off, and which countries and scientists are fighting back to find cures.

Players see a dynamic world. They're able to see how their choices are literally changing the map in front of them. That's effective worldbuilding. They witness the conflict between the disease and humanity unfold. When I play *Plague Inc.* and see a beaker pop up because a country's started research, I can picture in my imaginations the scientists gathered in a lab. The *game* doesn't need to give me a cutscene or even an image of this. It does a great job of showing the dynamic changes happening globally, and so my imagination adds details.

The game gives players strong, coded visuals of what's happening in the world. Ships and planes carry the disease from infected countries into healthy nations. Their travel routes trail behind them in red, the game's color for signifying infection. The goal is to cover the entire map, the entire *world*, in that blood red. A bloody, red world means the death of all humanity. As infected airplanes and ships travel back and forth, players can see the direct influence of their disease on the world. Whenever a country works on a cure, a "cure bubble" pops up. This is a blue icon with a lab beaker. Tapping the cure bubble and "popping" it slows down scientists' efforts to make a cure. Players also see the cure spreading from country to country. A large, blue airplane leaves one country on the map and flies to another, streaking a blue trail behind it. This is in strong contrast to all of the red infection trails planes and ships carrying the disease leave behind.

Little by little, blood-red pixel by blood-red pixel, the map fills up with infection. There's a sense of triumph when one of the last infected countries, usually a difficult to reach island, receives one of those red ships or planes, and a sense of defeat when they lock down their airports and seaports without a single person in the country being infected.

The player's imagination and emotions

Engaged imaginations make emotional connections. Animations create a sense of urgency through their movement and sudden appearances. There's a sense of urgency when cure bubbles start popping up all over the place. Even though killing off the planet instills a sense of achievement within me, I'm still horrified when a nation's government decides to execute its infected to keep the disease from spreading.

And how dare nations close down seaports and airports to stop the spread of disease! How dare nations research cures and spread medications throughout the world! *How dare* the world try to fight back and save humanity from extinction! I can see my actions and the world's counteractions in real time, which creates a sense that I have a very active villain fighting my efforts.

The game engages me with visuals and animations, but it's also pleasing in a tactile way as I tap the screen. It's *soooo* satisfying to "burst" cure bubbles, slowing down the race for the cure, and to tap DNA and mutation icons that help me strengthen the disease.

Plague Inc. is high drama—at least it is in my head.

getting the entire team involved with story delivery

If you've worked in games before, you know that getting any project released is a collaborative undertaking, unless you're working on every part of the game all by yourself. Narrative designers are facilitators—we're responsible for encouraging the rest of the team to contribute to the game's narrative design and story delivery. This means that we'll sometimes have to prove to our teammates that *they* are storytellers, and their unique skill sets are perfect for impacting the game's story delivery.

As illustrated through both *Mystery Match* and *Plague Inc.*, there are so many nontraditional ways to communicate a game's story and world. The following members of any team influence and contribute to a game's narrative design and story delivery:

- programmers/engineers/scripters,
- game designers,
- level designers,
- artists (concept, character, background, 2D/3D, etc.),
- UI designers,
- animators,
- sound designers,
- composers,
- narrative designers, and
- game writers.

Depending on a mobile and/or social game's requirements for story delivery, any or all of these disciplines may be involved.

Coming Up with a Plan

How do we get everyone involved, then? You'll need to come up with a narrative design plan that everyone understands and create an environment where they feel free to contribute and improve upon that plan. The fun thing about collaborating is that you have no idea how far someone can take your original concept. Because it's their area of expertise, what they come up with might be 10 times better than you would have ever thought.

First, you're going to need to understand the technical constraints you're working with. Team members responsible for programming will be able to tell you this. Does the game support 2D or 3D art? How many sound assets can you have? These are some of the kinds of questions you'll need answered because they will affect the game's story delivery.

Studios and clients have different processes for how they implement a game's narrative design. This means that *when* they bring in the narrative designer or narrative design team varies. If you really want your game's narrative design to be as strong as it can be, have a narrative designer and/or writer in place *when you start working on the game.* (Or, if you're wearing several hats, and one of them is "narrative designer," start working on your game's story delivery from the beginning of your development cycle.) It's common practice to bring in the narrative designer in the middle or even at the end of a game's development. However, this will make it even harder to implement nontraditional story features into the game, and you may discover you don't have the time or resources to incorporate some narrative design ideas. For example, you're working on a hidden-object game set in the Ancient Egyptian afterlife (Duat). Each level of the game takes place in one of the 12 regions of Duat. The narrative designer joins the team toward the end of the project. She suggests that the menus themselves can change from level to level to reflect each region as the player progresses. This will not only serve as a small reward for the player's success, but it will also be a part of the game's worldbuilding. Everyone thinks this is a great idea. There's just one problem. The UI designer has already finished the menus. Going back to redesign them will take too much time and cost more money when it's not in the budget.

conclusion

When narrative designers plan with the team at the start of the project, they're able to work with everyone to see what is and is not possible for the game, according to scope, budget, technical constraints, design, and schedule. As a narrative designer, you're a facilitator who encourages the entire team to contribute to the project's narrative design. You can use the concept of *story delivery* to help team members who don't believe they have storytelling skills see how their valuable expertise improves the game's narrative design.

the story delivery checklist

At the end of each chapter, you'll find a checklist to help you think about implementing the ideas you read. Let's start out with how you can make sure players always feel they're the driving force behind a mobile game's story, whether that story is a major part of the gameplay experience or only reflected in the mechanics.

> *Come up with a plan for story delivery with the entire team.* You won't be able to execute the game's narrative design without knowing the constraints you're working with. Once you understand those, you'll want to encourage all of your team members to use the entire game space, including the touchscreen, to tell the story.
>
> *Use all of the game's features as much as you're able.* Every part of the game has the potential for storytelling.
>
> *Use the player's imagination as a storytelling tool.* Player agency is key. Think of ways you can use players' imaginations to keep them connected and engaged to player characters, mechanics, and/or the story.
>
> *Remember that you don't always have to show—suggesting is sometimes enough.* You don't have to show players everything, nor do they have to experience everything. Suggesting is enough. Let their imaginations do the rest.

tips for working with the development team

(Chapters may also end with some quick tips to focus your writing or revision.)

- Discuss with the members of the team how the game can encourage and facilitate player agency.
- Discuss with game designers how to give narrative explanations for mechanics.
- Decide whether the game needs more traditional story delivery techniques, like cutscenes and dialogue trees.
- Use environmental narrative to communicate with players whenever possible.
- Look for ways to deliver story via nonstory features of the game.

from musical mechanics to emotional beats
story for nonstory games

Elizabeth LaPensée, PhD and Betsy Brey

contents

introduction

Game stories are a traditional mainstay of the console market, but in the mobile market, flexibility is key. We can't expect players to devote the same kind of dedicated, focused gaming time when they seek a game they can play on the go. The kinds of heavy-handed plot-development tricks used in consoles for 30 years, like text explanations or cutscenes, can stop a mobile game right in its tracks. A number of very successful mobile games sidestep storytelling as a whole and focus purely on nonstory gameplay, such as the dominant genres of puzzle/match-3 games or casino and slot machine mobile games. However, mobile developers should not be so quick to give up on story—we just need to rethink our strategies and how we approach story in mobile games. Whereas console games may often be driven by the story, mobile games can be nonstory driven. These are games that still build up an arc in gameplay but do not rely on story to do so. Nonetheless, these games are not entirely without story. Story can be conveyed in many ways, such as visual choices, audio, and mechanics. When it comes to mobile games, expressing narrative comes with not only limitations, but also opportunities.

Working around the constraints of mobile games can be challenging. Mobile games have to be smaller in scope than console games due to the smaller and limited storage capacities of mobile devices. Most developers counter this by making smaller, more focused games. Additionally, as mentioned earlier, mobile games are often played in small periods of downtime, meaning mobile games have to be easily sectioned or have natural breaks in gameplay structures, so users can pick up where they left off last time. The mobile marketplace is also dominated by free-to-play monetization strategies, making consumers skeptical of games that charge up front. The trickle stream of freemium models means developers need a lot of downloads to become successful, meaning the game must appeal to a wide audience. However, these unique constraints can create unique games, and we should view these factors as opportunities rather than limitations. Much like playing a game, the rules help guide our actions rather than overpower our experiences. As Christy Marx shares, "Writing for games is like writing haiku."* The structures in place help us create something new, especially when it comes to conveying story in nonstory-oriented games. Focusing on emotional connection, visuals, sound, and mechanics not only overcomes these limitations, but also tells a story without relying on text or cutscenes.

In Brenda Romero's series of analog games, mechanics of gameplay and the interaction between players are foundational to conveying meaning. In addition to using visual aspects of design to contribute to the story, she includes a deliberately provocative leading tell about the intention in her games through the mechanic that decides whose turn is first. Romero reiterates through her work that the mechanic is the message. In mobile gaming in particular, using mechanics to

---

* E-mail message to authors, March 23, 2016.

send a message helps overcome development constraints. Looking at two nonstory-oriented games, *Ephemerid: A Musical Adventure* and *Gemini*, we focused on examining the role of game mechanics as a way to express narrative and meet the expectations of mobile markets without sacrificing gameplay or story. In interviews with each game's developer(s), we found that meaningful mechanics not only encourage users to play and continue playing, but when designed with care, they can also tell a story at the same time.

interview #1: Matt Meyer

Interview 1: Ephemerid: A Musical Adventure (SuperChop Games, 2015)

> **How would you describe the core mechanics? Do these usually lend to narrative, or did you need to make adjustments?**

> **Matt Meyer:** The simplest way we like to describe *Ephemerid* is as a "musical adventure." It has mechanical elements of many genres (puzzle, point and click, rhythm), all meant to serve the music and story. We took special care to introduce/escalate these mechanics in such a way that the pacing of the game ebbs and flows along with the story. But most importantly, *Ephemerid* was designed around the ideas that music is the driving force of all the mechanics design and that the game mechanics must be designed in such a way that they are friendly to the player and can be learned through intuitive observation and experimentation.

> "Friendly" is not a typical word used to describe game mechanics but, again, we feel this was an important part of drawing the player into the story and helping them empathize with the main character. Really, "sympathize" is a better word, as we've always thought of the player as a third person in the story, not acting as the Ephemerid, but helping along its journey. There are many ways that *Ephemerid* is designed to be friendly to the player. One good example is that the music never changes according

to player input. It was important to me that we avoid the typical sort of punishment of discordant notes, loss of "points," or stopping the music altogether that most music games have when a player takes an undesirable action.

Screenshot from *Ephemerid: A Musical Adventure*. Developed/published by SuperChop Games and is protected by United States and international copyright law. © SuperChop Games

How did you integrate story into this genre of game?

Matt: We had a rough idea of the overarching story that we wanted to tell from pretty early on. But how we told that story came almost entirely from the principle of music first. For most of the development of *Ephemerid*, I would write a piece of music, and then Brent and I would sit down and spend a few days listening to the music piece and designing gameplay around it. This would sometimes take several iterations before landing on a scene/mechanic/ gameplay element that fit just right with what was needed for the music, story, and pacing.

We worked hard at making *Ephemerid* tell an engaging story without any words. It may have required extra work to do so but, ultimately, the game benefits by being more welcoming and friendly in that sense. The entire story is communicated through the universal languages of music, visuals, and touch. One of the many inspirations for the game was the movie *WALL-E*. In particular, the beautiful early sequences in the movie that are entirely without words and yet powerful and emotional.

What challenges did you face in creating narrative for a game like this? And how did you overcome them?

Matt: *Ephemerid* was a very challenging game to produce because we put difficult limits on what it would be (and, in many instances, what we didn't want it to be). No words, no tutorializing, no punishment for incorrect actions, no abstract indicators of when/where/how to interact (think of the collapsing circles found in many rhythm games used to indicate when the beat will hit). In essence, nothing that could pull the user out of the flow/story. We overcame these obstacles mostly with a lot of hard work and iteration.

There are entire scenes, mechanics, art environments, and songs that were pulled from the game because we never found a way to meet those core requirements. Throughout the game's development, I would bring *Ephemerid* to coffee shops and even strangers on the street (I literally hung out at a bus stop for several hours one day handing an iPad to passersby). There were times when some people would simply get stuck or frustrated. We'd go back to the drawing board and work on the scene or interaction until it was either fixed or simply needed to be discarded.

As we progressed into the development of *Ephemerid*, we were lucky enough to show at many large events with even more players eager to try out games. After each event, we'd have a better idea of what was really connecting with people and why. We could then go back and craft the experience even more.

Screenshot from *Ephemerid: A Musical Adventure*. Developed/published by SuperChop Games and is protected by United States and international copyright law. © SuperChop Games

What advice would you share about narrative strategies for nonstory-driven games?

Matt: Emotion was key for us in telling the story of *Ephemerid*. Treating the mechanics as a friend to the player will do wonders for engaging them in the story and not breaking the continuity. Most of the time, when the player is fighting against the game's mechanics, they are becoming less invested in the story. Many developers will only ever treat music as a second-class citizen in their games, but there are times when changing elements in order to better serve the music will dramatically improve the feel and narrative.

Lastly, having a high-level idea for the story we wanted to tell was instrumental in being able to craft that story. White boards (and more specifically storyboards) were a simple but essential tool throughout development.

interview #2: Atlas Chen and Nick Zhang

Interview 2: Gemini: A Journey of Two Stars (Echostone Games, 2016)

How would you describe the core mechanics? Do these usually lend to narrative, or did you need to make adjustments?

Atlas Chen: The core mechanism is that when the two stars are together, both can fly. The player controls the bigger one of the two stars, while the little star responds to its movement and the environment.

Intrinsically, this simple mechanism already shows some rich layers of metaphorical meanings. However, to achieve the drama we want, we did have a lot of tweaks on the little star's behavior, so that it feels alive and its character keeps evolving and growing as the story progresses.

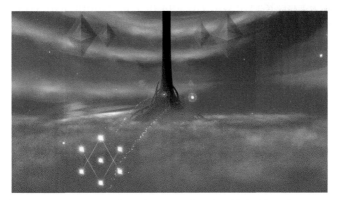

Screenshot from *Gemini: A Journey of Two Stars*. Developed/published by Echostone Games and is protected by United States and international copyright law. © Echostone Games

How did you integrate story into this genre of game?

Atlas: Instead of integrating story into a game as an afterthought, the game is designed based on the story, or more accurately, the emotional curve. *Gemini* is designed top-down. We decided our design goals and our artistic visions that we wanted to express through the game first. Then we worked on the story. It's a very typical narrative design: we built a background for the world setting, defined the conflicts and the motivations of the characters at the beginning and the end. We drew a drama curve for the emotional intensities. We crafted the plot points based on our adaptation of The Hero's Journey pattern. And we figured out the emotional beats, the specific moments that deliver the twist and revealing of information about the world, the characters, and their relationship. After that, we synthesized the story with graphics, music, and gameplay elements that can support the specific emotional impacts we wanted to deliver. We had a roadmap for all these elements for each story beat, to make sure they resonated with each other.

There are, of course, back-and-forth iterations when we hit a wall on the gameplay development and went back to change the story and even refined our top-down goals, but it was very important to have the big picture at the beginning so that we didn't get lost in the weeds. That approach really helped us make *Gemini* a cohesive narrative experience.

We tried to use minimal UI, texts, and cutscenes to tell the story, for we want to honor the unique way that games convey narrative—procedural presentation, storytelling by the rules, and gameplay dynamics. Unlike traditional media, the player makes choices in games, and I believe that makes the experience more impactful. As a game designer, I wanted to explore this strength. In screenwriting we say "show, don't tell"; in game design, we say "play, don't show."

What challenges did you face in creating narrative for a game like this? And how did you overcome them?

Nick Zhang: The first thing that comes to my mind is the tutorial; it is so difficult to teach players without text. Actually, at the prototype version of *Gemini*, we used to have a one-sentence tutorial: "When we are together, we feel we can fly." It works well. However, after a while, we decide to go totally non-text storytelling, so we decided not to show this sentence until the player sticks on the ground for too long, and then we have to spend months to adjust the movement and level design so that the gameplay itself is intuitive, and players can learn from the visual language or the movement of the little star.

Atlas: We challenged ourselves to create an NPC that feels alive. The challenge is that you want an NPC that feels alive while [it] is not too annoying. In traditional game design, most games' NPC allies are either easy to control to the extent that it feels like a tool rather than a life (e.g., a hostage in *Counter-Strike*) or never drag back the player (e.g., Elizabeth in *BioShock Infinite*). In *Gemini*, the little star is neither. To make sure the player still can play the game, the little star's response to the player's movement needs to be intuitive and learnable. To make it feel alive, it can't be repetitive. These goals require it to have its own goals and desires, avoidance to harms, awareness, and responses to environment, expressions of its feelings, a certain degree of predictable traits, and character growth.

Telling a story without text is another big challenge for us. We need to test it with real players to know if they get it and how much emotional impact the game delivers. It's very hard to test the narrative and emotion before the game is polished. The feedback you can get in early stages are mostly bugs, usability problems, and difficulty balance issues. Instead of making levels one by one, we had a full game running within the first two days of prototyping and started putting art and music into the project very early in development. Then we spent most of the rest of development time to iterate and polish.

Screenshot from *Gemini: A Journey of Two Stars*. Developed/published by Echostone Games and is protected by United States and international copyright law. © Echostone Games

What advice would you share about narrative strategies for non-story-driven games?

Atlas: *Gemini* is a unique, experimental project. We can't say our practice is the best for this kind of game since there aren't many yet. But we do have some lessons that we can share.

One thing we greatly benefit from is reflecting on ourselves and being honest. What really matters to us? What is it that we wanted to express as an artist? Having a clear purpose and writing it down helped us move forward quickly with a lot of otherwise arbitrary design decisions. There can be so many possibilities when you are trying to tell a story. You need a goal, a single vision, to unify the team's direction.

Storytelling without words and with gameplay is challenging and expensive, but it can be very meaningful because every player can have a very personal interpretation to the story, which reflects who they are. Without words, it's very hard to deliver a complicated plot. But maybe that is its strength. We tried to figure out what is the fundamental emotion that all men share. Being general and abstract means that more people can relate to the story. We had thousands of players reviewing the game and writing down their own versions of the stories with very different interpretations of the metaphor of the relationship between the two stars. All of them are very beautiful and personal.

It's good to have details and cohesive background stories. It helps us to create a cohesive experience with rich details to discover. But I would suggest focusing on the emotion, the drama, the big picture. That is what really matters to the player's experience. To achieve this, good pacing is a key. And you would need a ton of playtests. We tested the game with hundreds of players before its final version.

discussion

So, what do these interviews suggest about designing mobile game stories? We all know playtesting often and early makes for better games, but consistent and early playtesting with a variety of players is crucial for creating a nonstory-driven mobile game. Both teams said this kind of design is hard to do because of the amount of playtesting and iteration—which comes at the cost of development time and additional hours of work—but it is impossible to see how players respond without it. *Gemini's* Atlas discusses how difficult it is to get story feedback early in playtesting because in the first few iterations of a game, players tend to focus on bugs, usability problems, and difficulty balance rather than anything else. To work around this, *Gemini*'s team created the full game within a few days of prototyping, instead of making levels one by one. This allowed the team to add the art and music into the game early, giving them time to focus heavily on polishing and playtesting new iterations, and ensuring that player response and movement in the game were intuitive and easy to learn. Matt from *Ephemerid* mentions bringing various versions of the game to coffee shops and bus stops, asking strangers if they would playtest the game. If people got stuck or frustrated, the design team would take it back to the drawing board, focus back on their core mission and goals, and playtest again. Having numerous kinds of players with different backgrounds, expectations, and background knowledge is very helpful to seeing how intuitive the game is to players.

To achieve this level of early and constant playtesting, you need to know what your story goals are before you start prototyping. Designing the story first, rather than mechanics or genre, helps streamline your workflow and keep your design team focused throughout the process. Having a high-level idea for the story from the start helped keep the team focused throughout playtesting cycles. *Ephemerid's* Matt notes that storyboards "were a simple but essential tool throughout development." *Gemini's* developers used a similar tactic. Atlas says, "We had a roadmap for all these elements for each story beat, to make sure they resonate with each other," and details the process of creating the narrative at the beginning of the development:

1. Build the background.
2. Establish conflicts.
3. Define character motivation at both the beginning and the end of the story.
4. Outline the drama curve for emotional intensities—high points, low points that are situated evenly to pace the game.
5. Craft plot points fitting the drama curve—when information (about the characters, the world, the relationships in the world, etc.) is revealed.

Matt echoes the emphasis that the emotional intensities are crucial in nonstory-driven games, as they are signposts for players' emotional responses. Often referred to as "beats" in writing, small moments of change in emotion, action, or character's relationships and joining together for larger-scale changes that direct the plot. Taking a deeper look, emotional beats, meaning key emotionally driven points in a story, can help players understand the arc of the game through their own experience. Importantly, the pacing of emotions can make or break the player's experience, and having the main ideas prepared early ensures that the emotional intensities are present and balanced; you don't want to have too much emotional buildup in any one single part of the game. Too much emotional intensity at the beginning of the game means players can be overwhelmed, but not enough early in the game will not engage players and motivate them to keep playing. The storyboard process helps ensure emotional and dramatic balance in the game. These emotional beats, or small, individual emotional responses and actions within a character's growth in the story, should be considered when designing nonstory games. Building emotional beats can be as detailed as creating mini storyboards for character development within the plot, in addition to wider plot storyboarding.

This kind of storyboard process is also helpful for development teams to stay focused during iterative development cycles. It helped the *Gemini* team decide what was important to the game and the team early. Not only does that help the team create a cohesive story with interesting and meaningful details, but it also allows the design team something to look back on throughout the long playtesting cycles—a point of unity and a goal to help simplify later choices about how to adapt and work with feedback about the game.

Something both *Gemini's* and *Ephemerid's* development teams decided early in their design processes was that story was important to the game, but doing so in a way that supports gameplay was more important than a precise, exact narrative. In the interview, Atlas plainly states, "without words, it's very hard to deliver a complicated plot," but both *Gemini* and *Ephemerid* choose to create an experience and a setting for emotions rather than the kind of complicated plots we might see in games with cutscenes. The strength of this kind of storytelling, though, is that it allows players to have their own personal interpretations of the story. Atlas also points out that screenwriting has the golden rule "show, don't tell," but game story design revolves around the idea "play, don't show." Matt discusses how *Ephemerid* accomplishes this through music, visuals, and touch. *Gemini* focuses mostly on emotions and feelings that help players relate to the story. But both design teams focused on making the mechanics work, not just functionally, but also emotionally and narratively.

After we look over the developers' responses to the interview questions, the importance of mechanics in nonstory-driven games becomes clear. When the player experiences a game without the usual narrative trappings of cutscenes or text explanations, the mechanics are crucial because they are the driving force of the player's inter-action with the game. They can't be covered up or smoothed over with a quick cutscene or dialogue box—they must be intuitive, and engaging and, most importantly, the actions performed in playing the game must suit the tone, story, and gameplay dynamics. If the actions afforded by the game's mechanics don't match or compliment other parts of the game, players will struggle to connect with the game and the story. Matt from the *Ephemerid* design team referred to trying their game's mechanics as "friendly," explaining that when players have to fight against the grain to operate the mechanics, they also struggle to connect the mechanics to the story. He explains that "treating the mechanics as a friend to the player will do wonders for engaging them in the story and not breaking the continuity," which helps players focus on the experience of the game. The more time players spend struggling with mechanics, the less time they spend becoming invested in the game.

Examples of ways to make your mechanics "friendly" to the player are ensuring that mechanics can be learned through intu-ition, observation, and experimentation. Matt explains this means "no words, no tutorializing, no punishment for incorrect actions, no abstract indicators of when/where/how to interact, nothing that could pull the user out of the flow/story." Although the *Gemini* devel-opers didn't use the word "friendly" to describe their mechanics, their design philosophies agree with the *Ephemerid* design team's goals. Nick from *Gemini* explains that the prototype originally included a sentence-long tutorial to get players started. However, they felt it worked against their design goals to have that sentence and wanted to make sure the learning process was more intuitive and welcom-ing to players, so the *Gemini* team instead focused on making sure players could learn from the visuals and movements of characters in the game, rather than a direct tutorial sentence. None of this is to suggest that "friendly" mechanics mean a game without challenge. Games with friendly mechanics can still be challenging—both *Gemini* and *Ephemerid* have challenging levels—but friendly mechanics mean that the player remains in sync with the gameplay experience.

They don't blame the game for their failures, but instead feel motivated to experiment and try a new strategy or approach to a level.

It's noteworthy that both development teams also discuss the importance of music in their designs for conveying emotion and story. Adding in the music early in the design helped guide *Gemini* throughout playtesting, and *Ephemerid* is a music-centered game, so the music guides the mechanics and experience. But Matt brings up an important point in nonstory-driven games. He explains that music is often considered later in the design process, treating music and audio as decorations rather than storytelling elements. When trying to tell a story without text, cutscenes, or intense UI elements, paying attention to the emotion and connection of key moments in the play experience and planning music and audio for those moments can go a long way for creating a lasting impression.

conclusion

At the end of all of this, there are a few main things we can take away about designing story for nonstory-driven games. While mobile games have unique constraints, we can look at those limitations as ways to help improve and change how we tell stories in games. Focusing on designing a story first and using the tone and style of the story to connect with players emotionally helps guide the design process. Music, visuals, and mechanics help ensure that players understand the story, even without the awkward, traditional narrative methods of cutscenes and textual exposition. Mechanics are crucial in nonstory-driven mobile games, because like Brenda Romero says, "the mechanic is the message"*—they are how the player interacts with and comes to understand the game. Last but not least, playtesting often with a large number of players, preferably ones who have not played a previous iteration of the game, helps make sure your game is intuitive, challenging, and engaging.

We would like to wrap up our discussion with a series of questions you can ask yourself and your development team. Storytelling and creating a story for a nonstory-driven game can be challenging, but players can connect with the game in personal, unique ways that make all the effort worth it.

---

* Brenda Romero, "The mechanic is the message," *The Mechanic Is the Message* (blog), published May 7, 2009, https://mechanicmessage.wordpress.com.

checklist

Are your mechanics "friendly"? Do they support the player, or does the player have to fight against them to play?

During playtesting, did you check in with your players about the story? Asking them to focus on that, rather than bugs, usability problems, difficulty, etc., can help focus playtesters in early stages of playtesting.

Were playtesters able to identify the emotional beats of the story? In what ways?

Have you playtested with players beyond your target audience or expected player base?

Did you consider how music interacts with the player's experience?

Is your game focused on a main story? Do you have a record or firm concept for the story that the team can look back on to help make decisions during later iterations and polishing?

How can you make sure your story follows the "play, don't tell" guideline? What parts of your game (text, UI, cutscenes) can you make playable, rather than merely instructional?

Do your mechanics make sense with the story concept? Do they help tell the story or main idea?

What other kinds of mechanics can you think of that might help tell a story more fully?

livable and believable, despite the limitations
worldbuilding

Toiya Kristen Finley, PhD

contents

When we think about worldbuilding in videogames, we conceptualize an interactive place where players can involve themselves with characters and environments. Sounds get their attention. Animations draw their eye, and they can interact with objects to solve puzzles or overcome obstacles. These places often give players the freedom of self-expression, whether they're building in the *Sims*, *SimCity*, or *Minecraft*. Or maybe their interactions with the world and its inhabitants lead to changes in that world, such as in the BioWare and Telltale franchises. Traditionally, players move about the world and effect changes through gameplay (such as destroying objects, exploring the environment, helping/harming NPCs, etc.). Or they affect the story (making choices that change the world on major and minor scales).

Mobile and social games with the technical capacity and budget can present worlds in the same manner as traditional videogames. They have multiple art assets for a variety of environments; set pieces, animations, and sound assets for mechanics, characters, and creatures; and cinematics and cutscenes. But *all* game worlds occupy a space, even if the space is only composed of a couple of screens. That means, as narrative designers, we need to make sure that the game's entire world fits in that space and feels like a well-developed, breathing place.

I mention in "Keeping the Player at the Heart of the Story" (Chapter 1) that the player's imagination is one of the (if not *the* most) powerful tools narrative designers and game writers have. Players don't need to see or be told everything in order to imagine it for themselves. We can give them enough to fill in the blanks. When it comes to worldbuilding, audiences (of book series, movies, and videogames) don't *need* to know everything. But let's say you *are* working on a game that's heavy on story. It's a hidden-object game with a setting based on the underworld of Ancient Egyptian mythology. You need to do your research, but you *still* don't need to communicate all of the features of this world to the player. While players may look for objects based on each hour as they pass through the underworld, they don't need to understand every single thing about the hours to understand the world they temporarily inhabit. Bogging them down with such details might, in fact, be *less* interesting to them.

When designing a world, we need to decide what players absolutely need to know about the places they're interacting with and how we can use various worldbuilding techniques to communicate them. These techniques aid in communicating both story and gameplay.

Worldbuilding is made up of history, cultures, locations, environmental narrative, religions, magic/technology/science systems, and languages. Depending on the project, we might develop all or only one of these categories. For example, for a clicker game, I might only need to design a few locations for the level design and art teams. For the Ancient Egyptian underworld game, I would need to flesh out religion, culture, locations, environmental narrative, and language:

- *Religion*: souls pass through one life to the next through the underworld.
- *Culture*: Ancient Egyptians believe how they live life will be mirrored in their afterlife.
- *Locations*: each hour (level) is a different part of Duat (the underworld).
- *Environmental narrative*: players figure out what they're looking for during each hour through interacting with the environment.
- *Language*: hieroglyphs are a fundamental part of Ancient Egyptian culture, and players will see hieroglyphic writing in the environment.

How we evoke a sense of the world's history and who/what inhabits it can be expressed through art, sound, animations, and mechanics—or simply in a few lines of text.

worldbuilding through environmental narrative

While the graphics may not be photorealistic and you may not get as many locations and levels to design, you can still communicate information about the world through the environment. *Environmental narrative* should communicate something to players, just as text does.

Through environmental narrative, the world expresses to the player different types of information about itself. That information can be about almost anything: characters, history, places, mechanics, puzzles, etc.

Let's say you're playing an RPG or action adventure. You happen upon a town, and all of the buildings are in piles of smoldering rubble. You know that someone or something has rushed in and destroyed that town. Furthermore, if all of the town's citizens are absent, you can guess that those people all fled or were killed. What's even more interesting is that you can hear something crackling. The sound leads you to the town square, where someone or something has gathered up hundreds of paintings from that town, dumped them in heaps in the middle of the town square, and lit them on fire. Whatever or whoever did this to the town had a reason for burning those paintings, and it could tell you something about a motive.

The above example may seem like a "Well, duh!" explanation, but everything you see in that town is environmental narrative telling you specific things about the world, *communicating* something to you: somebody destroyed the town, somebody may or may not have killed all of the town's inhabitants, and somebody had an important reason for torching hundreds of the town's paintings. In addition, you can probably deduce at least one of the town's characteristics—these people have a culture interested in art (all of those paintings).

Hide and Seek: Story of Dorothy: A Few Good Assets

This same kind of communication works in mobile games, whether they have 2D or 3D graphics. *Hide and Seek: Story of Dorothy* (2014, stylized as *HideAndSeek[Story of Dorothy]*) from TabomSoft is in the mold of the *Corpse Party* franchise. Dorothy, a young girl, wakes up in a closet after falling asleep playing a game of hide-and-seek. Trapped in a haunted house, she finds herself separated from her family. She must ultimately search for clues to discover what happened to her and best the game's antagonist. Players interact with the world to solve puzzles, read item descriptions, and talk to NPCs. As is the case with other RPGs, some items aren't necessary to solve puzzles, but they have descriptions through flavor text to add interest about player character Dorothy's surroundings and the world at large (for more on flavor text, see the section "Worldbuilding through Text" later in this chapter).

An important aspect to remember about worldbuilding is that it's not just visual. *Story of Dorothy* has a few animation and sound assets to go along with its visuals. The combination of animations, still visuals, and sound makes the world feel "lived in." They suggest that the world is alive and inhabited in places that aren't currently viewable on the screen.

The game uses sound effects sparingly and explains to players where those sounds are coming from. This is effective for a couple of reasons: (1) the fewer the assets, the less storage space the game requires (art and sound files take up the most storage space), and (2) the occasional sound effect signals "Hey, pay attention!" to players. The world establishes that sound is important and gives hints for puzzles and guides players as to where to go next. Because the sound isn't directional (i.e., players aren't going to hear sound to their right, left, in front, or behind), text accompanies sound clues.

Screenshot from *Hide and Seek: Story of Dorothy*. Developed/published by TabomSoft and is protected by United States and international copyright law. © TabomSoft

After players pick up the cutter machine, a sound effect and line of text alert them to a change in the world outside of the room. Screenshot from *Hide and Seek: Story of Dorothy*. Developed/published by TabomSoft and is protected by United States and international copyright law. © TabomSoft

These changes are important to the game's environmental narrative. A seemingly normal painting will transform into a bloody one. A couple of art assets accomplish this. It doesn't need to be animated with blood running down for the player to realize a painting has started to ooze blood. The eyes in portraits follow Dorothy as she walks past them. In a row of otherwise normal paintings, one will have a pool of blood underneath it, signaling that it's a death trap and players shouldn't try to interact with it.

Screenshot from *Hide and Seek: Story of Dorothy*. Developed/published by TabomSoft and is protected by United States and international copyright law. © TabomSoft

Although this transformation isn't animated, it's still plenty creepy. Screenshot from *Hide and Seek: Story of Dorothy*. Developed/published by TabomSoft and is protected by United States and international copyright law. © TabomSoft

In addition, the game doesn't show players everything and trusts their imaginations. Items are necessary for solving puzzles, and players need to collect them. Dorothy picks up items, but there are no art assets for them. They're listed in the inventory with no accompanying pictures. Players are simply told, "There is a match under the dusty doll," but they don't need to see the match to know that they've picked it up. If you don't need to spend storage space on assets, why create them? A line of text tells the player what the item is and describes anything that might be unique about it.

However, when the narrative design *does* include animations in the environment, it's all the more impactful because it's rare. Dorothy interacts with a ghost at a dinner setting. The game doesn't include a character model for the ghost. Instead, a spoon swirls in a bowl where the ghost sits. Again, no character model means conservation of storage space, but the spoon's movement allows the player to imagine what that ghost looks like. Seeing the spoon and not the ghost—while the ghost holds a conversation with Dorothy—is going to be more disturbing for some players.

Screenshot from *Hide and Seek: Story of Dorothy*. Developed/published by TabomSoft and is protected by United States and international copyright law. © TabomSoft

Environmental narrative, descriptions, and occasional, text-based NPC dialogue make it clear that this house had victims before Dorothy arrived. Blood spatters doors with death traps behind them, puddles of blood from past visitors stain floors and walls, and haunted paintings mock Dorothy by telling her they're surprised she's survived up until now.

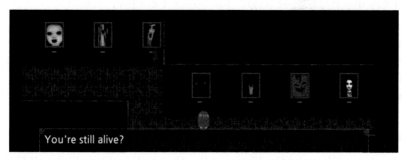

Screenshot from *Hide and Seek: Story of Dorothy*. Developed/published by TabomSoft and is protected by United States and international copyright law. © TabomSoft

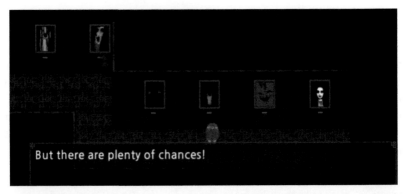

Screenshot from *Hide and Seek: Story of Dorothy*. Developed/published by TabomSoft and is protected by United States and international copyright law. © TabomSoft

A trio of ghost paintings taunts Dorothy and builds upon the house's hostile atmosphere. Screenshot from *Hide and Seek: Story of Dorothy*. Developed/published by TabomSoft and is protected by United States and international copyright law. © TabomSoft

This is a familiar haunted house setting, but it's an active, engaged world with a clear motive to torment Dorothy and keep her from her family.

worldbuilding through text

Another way players experience worldbuilding is by reading informational text, lore, and flavor text. Although we think of using text as potentially committing the cardinal writing sin of "telling, not showing," text is versatile and can enhance the storytelling experience. Also, it takes up next to nothing when it comes to a mobile device's storage.

Plague Inc.'s News Reports

In Chapter 1, "Keeping the Player at the Heart of the Story," I detail *Plague Inc.'s* (Ndemic Creations, 2012) dynamic worldbuilding. A real-time strategy game, *Plague Inc.* illustrates immediate, dynamic changes in the world through strong visual and tactile cues. The player's goal is to spread infection throughout the world and kill off all of humanity. At the same time, humanity fights back by closing down airports and seaports, killing diseased animals, burning infected corpses, and working feverishly (pun most definitely intended) on a cure.

Players evolve and devolve their disease in an effort to stay ahead of humanity's struggle to eradicate it. In this way, the visuals show players this back-and-forth action and reaction in real time on a map of the world. Planes and ships constantly travel across the map, journeying between nations. You'll know when the disease is successfully spreading because those planes and ships will turn red, and you'll witness where these vessels pick up the disease and where they'll travel as they transport it to infect another country. You can watch animated airplane and ship routes spread the disease as blood-red lines trail behind them. The disease also mutates, becoming more dangerous. Hazard symbols pop up in various places, showing players exactly where the mutations are happening. Beakers pop up on the world map, revealing that certain countries are working on a cure. Players can tap these beakers to destroy them and slow down scientists' efforts. Watching how their choices turn the map red, players literally see they're changing the world.

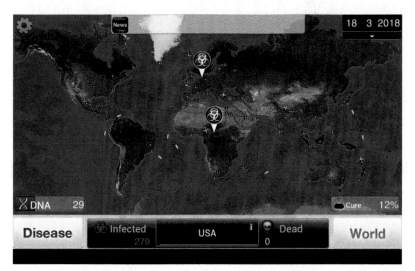

Early in its life, a bacterial disease mutates in Africa and Europe. Screenshot from *Plague Inc.* Developed/published by Ndemic Creations and is protected by United States and international copyright law. © Nedemic Creations

Plague Inc. uses text to highlight these dynamic changes. The text in the game has several roles:

- updates players on whether they're currently winning or losing,
- announces nations' actions in response to player actions, and
- gives bits of story and provide some humor.

Updates and announcements

The updates alert players as to how well their sessions are going. In other words, the game provides textual feedback telling players how well their disease is or isn't doing and if the world is effectively fighting back. Once players start making choices to evolve the disease, the world will respond. For example, players can make the disease waterborne. When countries discover ships are vectors for transmission, they shut down their seaports and quarantine themselves.

Screenshot from *Plague Inc.* Developed/published by Ndemic Creations and is protected by United States and international copyright law. © Nedemic Creations

One strategy is to keep the disease undetected for as long as possible and to lead countries to believe it isn't virulent. Once the world takes notice, it will begin working on a cure. This feedback shows up in text boxes players can't miss.

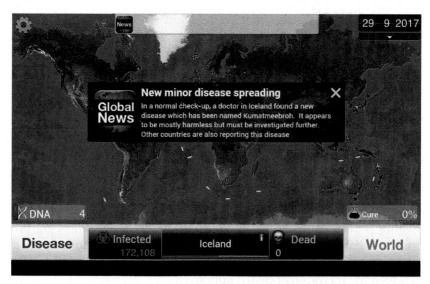

Detection leads to investigation. Screenshot from *Plague Inc.* Developed/published by Ndemic Creations and is protected by United States and international copyright law. © Nedemic Creations

As nations start to work on a cure, players will need to evolve the disease and make it easier to spread. Screenshot from *Plague Inc.* Developed/published by Ndemic Creations and is protected by United States and international copyright law. © Nedemic Creations

In the first screenshot, the disease begins in Iceland. Therefore, an Icelandic doctor discovers the new disease while examining a patient. It is important here to note that the game tailors these informational texts to the player's choices, and the dynamic worldbuilding influences the little bit of story the player receives.

Bits of story

Plague Inc. uses these vignette-like scenarios in the occasional event, as well. The in-world Global News presents the occasional event in headlines, mimicking actual news networks. These random story events can be serious or amusing.

The events also forecast the state of the world based upon the disease's pathology and rate of transmission. In the following play-through, as humanity nears extinction, even world leaders are ill. The chance for the human race's survival is dire. And societies break down as fear, terror, and death spread.

Screenshot from *Plague Inc.* Developed/published by Ndemic Creations and is protected by United States and international copyright law. © Nedemic Creations

Screenshot from *Plague Inc.* Developed/published by Ndemic Creations and is protected by United States and international copyright law. © Nedemic Creations

The Global News news ticker scrolls at the top center of the screen. The news may or may not be directly related to the disease's progress and the world's retaliation. Often, the news here is amusing. At the beginning of a game and before the disease turns deadly, there will be some news unrelated to the disease.

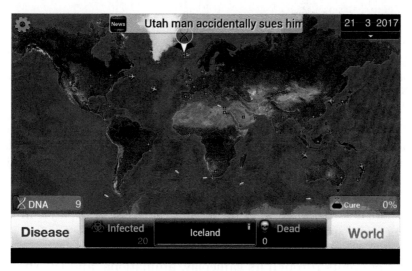

You need to laugh a little while destroying the world. Screenshot from *Plague Inc.* Developed/published by Ndemic Creations and is protected by United States and international copyright law. © Nedemic Creations

While the game provides humor and fleshes out what's happening in the world, the news ticker is still a part of *Plague Inc.'s* dynamic worldbuilding. Global News becomes more and more attentive of the disease—until it becomes Global News's only focus—as the world's situation grows grimmer.

Lastly, *Plague Inc.* has subtle, effective story delivery through its UI's narrative design. You've probably already noticed the UI at the bottom of the screenshots. Counters labeled "Infected" and "Dead" display these numbers on either side of a country. Players can choose individual countries to display, and a meter goes from blue to red as that population dies, or from red to blue as the cure spreads.

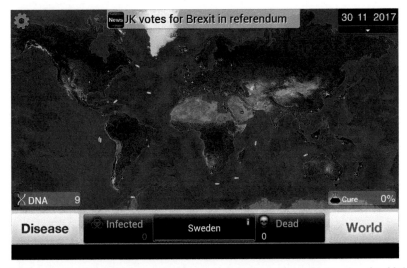

No deaths in Sweden. No deaths anywhere. Drat. Screenshot from *Plague Inc.* Developed/published by Ndemic Creations and is protected by United States and international copyright law.
© Nedemic Creations

The numbers go up and down in real time, so players can see the death toll climb or the number of infected people decrease. The fact that players can watch these numbers change heightens the excitement as players race to keep pushing up the death toll, and increases the dismay when those numbers slow down and stop. The fluctuating numbers add to the dynamic aspect of the changes the player inflicts on the world and the world's determination to right itself.

Not a story-oriented game by any means, *Plague Inc.* narrates a series of events through its gameplay, animations, and UI. The bits of story it does give provide context to world events and the player's decisions.

DragonSoul's Lore and Flavor Text

Lore is the mythology of a world or culture. It can cover every aspect of that world, including history, religion, art, music, literature, architecture, locations, and people. It is usually found in the books and letters lying around in the worlds of RPGs and action adventures.

Lore is also versatile because you can use it in any game, whether the game's story-oriented or not. If you're working on a game that has technical limitations or isn't story-oriented, you can express what the world's like through its lore. It's just enough of a "taste" to give players a general idea. A diversity of lore teaches players about different aspects of the world. Lore can appear anywhere. Character bios, menus, and skill/weapon descriptions are all places where you can insert it.

You'll often place lore in *flavor text*. Flavor text is brief and adds some interest to nonstory information. Stat screens, skill trees, and other menus that provide information on mechanics or gameplay might have lines of flavor text. The flavor text connects that information to the world of the game. For example, information about a laptop item's abilities will have a line about the famed hacker who once used it.

You can write lore and flavor text in any style or tone to fit the game's aesthetic. These can be poetry, jokes, journal entries, advertisements, pamphlets—whatever you need to communicate about a certain aspect of the world (a location, character, creature, weapon, etc.).

DragonSoul (Fantasy Legend Studios/GREE, 2015) is a mobile game with a plot that advances through its story campaign. An evil dragon, Umlaut, has taken over the land, and a group of heroes band together to defeat him. As players collect heroes, they can choose which ones to include in the party to advance through the story and other game modes. Players must level up to progress to each new chapter. While the game has a definite plot, there's not much character development through the story itself. Players learn about the heroes in the game through lore and flavor text. This includes tidbits about their hobbies, rivalries, friendships, and exploits. The game is humorous and loves its pop cultural references, which often come out in the flavor text.

Look at these stats for Dark Dracul, one of *DragonSoul's* heroes. The paragraph at the top is flavor text with some lore sprinkled in. We get some information about Dracul himself (and the fate of his trusting guests), but we also learn that there is TV and news media in this world.

Screenshot from *DragonSoul*. © 2018 Fantasy Legend Studios, Inc. All rights reserved.

When writing lore and flavor text,

- consider what aspects of the world the player needs to learn about or might find interesting,
- think about where flavor text can appear in the game, and
- choose writing styles and tones that fit the game's aesthetic and world.

worldbuilding through game modes

Game modes are an opportunity to show players different parts of the world, especially if you're working on a game with a small budget or a mobile game. In AAA titles, players will be interacting in multiple environments throughout the game. However, even with limited budgets and technology, we have some tricks to make the world feel larger.

Art assets can suggest different places in the world. You can discuss with the team lead, game designer, and art team what background art you would use for these locations. Each game mode can have its own location. Where does it make sense for these modes to happen in the world? Can you pull locations from the worldbuilding you've already done, or do you need to create new ones? If you can reuse art assets, this saves space and helps to decrease production time.

DragonSoul has a variety of game modes. Among them are

- Campaign—progressing through the story,
- The Mountain—looting health potions and ore (in-game currency),
- Challenges—fighting specific types of enemies,
- Crypt—competing against a set number of other players' teams with one's guild,
- Fight Pit—competing against other players' teams (one at a time) to progress through fighting divisions,
- Coliseum—competing against other players' teams (one team in three rounds) to progress through fighting divisions,
- Expedition—fighting 15 players' teams as they progress in level and difficulty,
- Temple—fighting five "Titan-sized" heroes with the help of guild members,
- Boss Pit—fighting against three bosses with different abilities, and
- Guild War—competing with one's guild against a set number of players in another guild.

Additionally, the game often runs contests. The instructions and reward notifications include in-world flavor text with story scenarios or messages from the heroes themselves.

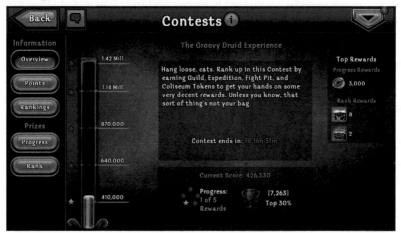

This contest features Groovy Druid, a hippyish elf. Screenshot from *DragonSoul*. © 2018 Fantasy Legend Studios, Inc. All rights reserved.

With so many game modes, *DragonSoul* uses different 2D background art to represent the different locations where the modes take place. The Mountain has "The Summit" for looting potions and "The Caves" for ores, representing different parts of the mountain where the heroes travel. The Crypt is where Umlaut raises dead heroes, and the Boss Pit features enemy NPCs whom Umlaut has swayed by his influence. Each of the bosses has their own location. The visual representations for these modes also help to suggest the feeling of being in different places in the world. With all of the locations used in the backgrounds, it feels like the player's traveling the world through these modes. And *DragonSoul* does an excellent job of reusing its background assets. For example, some of the locations for the boss pits also appear in the story campaign. The heroes are chasing down the bosses to engage them in combat, so it makes sense that they would journey through places they've been before.

By adding flavor text and/or lore to a mode's description or instructions, you give context for the mode that's based in the world. The mode feels less like something else to do in the game apart from the story campaign when we can ground it in a scenario. Here are some of the Crypt's instructions:

> Umlaut is raising Heroes from the Crypts. Wipe out his possessed legions before they overwhelm the land!*

Every part of the game uses the opportunity to express what the world is like through flavor text—even descriptions for alternative skins. The effect is that players are constantly immersed in the world of *DragonSoul*. Everything about it is consistent with the world's tone and aesthetic.

Incorporating Worldbuilding into Game Modes

Here are a few things to consider if you're working on a game with different modes.

- Can the mode be situated somewhere in the game's world?
- Can art visually represent the mode as a place situated in the world?

---

* *DragonSoul*, Fantasy Legend Studios (2015; Madison, WI: GREE.), Videogame.

- Can you add flavor text/lore to the mode's instructions or information to make the worldbuilding feel more immersive?
- Do you have a variety of locations, including interior and exterior (if applicable)?

Worldbuilding through Mechanics and Gameplay: *DragonSoul*

Mechanics

Sometimes worldbuilding can explain the gameplay itself. In *DragonSoul*, players collect heroes with different stats and skills and level them up. At the beginning of the game, players have two heroes, Unstable Understudy and Dragon Lady. They unlock a third, Centaur of Attention, after completing the tutorial. After that, players unlock heroes randomly by collecting each hero's soulstones or receiving a hero automatically by opening chests. Players acquire soulstones through chests and different types of shops that have specialized in-game currency. How long it takes to unlock each hero will be unique to each player. A star system categorizes heroes by rarity: one star (requires 10 soulstones to unlock), two stars (requires 30 to unlock), and three stars (requires 80 to unlock). Whether players have unlocked a certain hero or not, that hero may show up in the game's cutscenes. Since the team of heroes is collecting more allies as they go, this supports the *story* happening in the world, while it may not be the exact experience in individual player's games.

Additionally, during the story campaign, players discover that Umlaut possesses heroes through their soulstones. So, they're fighting on the side of evil against their will. When new heroes appear in the story, their eyes glow green to show they're possessed, and they battle the players' "good guys" who are working together to defeat Umlaut. Also, players can encounter possessed heroes they've already acquired. Actually, this happens quite often. The game's worldbuilding gives an explanation through its lore.

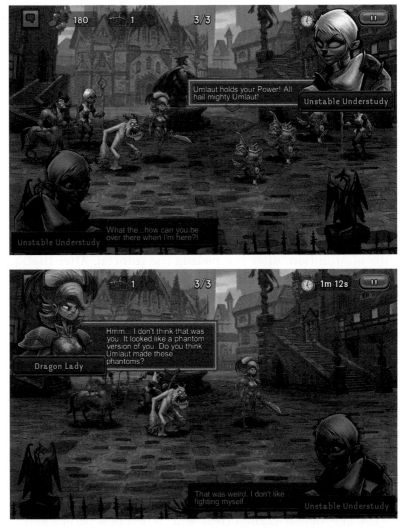

Screenshots from *DragonSoul.* © 2018 Fantasy Legend Studios, Inc. All rights reserved.

The soulstones themselves, the things players need to acquire, are the key to this strange phenomenon. Early on, Unstable Understudy sees the doppelganger of herself with glowing green eyes. How is this possible? Umlaut uses the soulstones to make these phantoms. Therefore, no matter the heroes the player has acquired, an evil version may show up somewhere in the story campaign or other modes to fight them.

This worldbuilding technique makes sense for a game where players' experiences are diverse and influenced by randomization.

Giving some backstory or a magical/technological scenario explains away player experiences that may be divergent from the game's story.

Gameplay

You can build a world in mobile games through traditional means, too. As I mentioned above, *DragonSoul* has cutscenes. Characters converse through portraits and text boxes. These usually pop up before the third stage of a fight. While there are visuals (each stage has a specific location and accompanying art), characters often drop nuggets about the world they live in and hint at things you can't see. (This is the same technique *Mystery Match* uses. See Chapter 1, "Keeping the Player at the Heart of the Story.")

Screenshot from *DragonSoul*. © 2018 Fantasy Legend Studios, Inc. All rights reserved.

socializing the world: nintendo's streetpass games

Games' social mechanics also make their worlds feel large and dynamic beyond what players see on their own screens. There are other inhabitants of the same world having their own adventures. This is a common concept for MMOs, but it's also possible for social games, whether they're online or mobile.

Social games tend to have an element where players trade resources and energy/stamina or visit each other's cities/houses in games like *The Sims Social* or the *FarmVille* franchise. A major reason why players need to have as many friends as possible playing the game is because they can get daily rewards from these friends. More friends mean they progress more quickly through the game. In this way, friends are also resources. But the scenarios going on in the world can provide other reasons for adding friends and having them interact in each other's games.

Although they're not mobile *technically*, the Nintendo 3DS StreetPass games *are* social games. When players carry their 3DSs and are in the same vicinity, the 3DS consoles SpotPass. The SpotPass transfers data over Wi-Fi from 3DS console to 3DS console, and the 3DSs collect players' Mii information. Miis are customizable player characters the StreetPass games use. Through SpotPass, those Miis become available in other people's games.

In the StreetPass games, other players' Miis are directly involved in the world's story. In fishing game *Ultimate Angler* (Prope, 2015), the player character visits a local fishing clubhouse and makes a fishing trip with guide character Coraline (for more on guide characters, please see Chapter 4, "Not Just Tutorial Hosts: Characters"). After the first trip out to sea, a legendary sea monster rocks the player character's boat, spilling all of the bait in the water. Coraline informs the PC that guests to the clubhouse usually bring their own bait, so she doesn't sell any. This provides the need to acquire more Miis: the Miis are visitors going to the clubhouse to fish. When they find out the player doesn't have any bait, they gift bait to the player upon their arrival. So, if there are 10 guests, the player receives 10 pieces of bait. Players also can choose what color clothes their Miis wear. The type of bait Miis give is color-coordinated and based upon their clothes. Fish have bait preferences. It behooves players to gather as many Miis as possible because they'll need a variety of bait. Better variety brings better opportunities to catch fish.

Miis' usefulness doesn't end there. The fish in the game are of varying sizes and difficulties to catch. The larger the fish, the more help players need reeling them in. The largest/rare fish or legendary monsters are a lot easier to catch when there are 10 Miis to help, instead of 2 or 3.

Ultimate Angler puts a spin on other players visiting a game session by creating a scenario for them to help a player. These Miis are visiting the clubhouse, interested in the same activity as the player.

They're helping out a fellow angler in need by giving bait. Additionally, it's common for multiple customers to go on fishing tours together. Therefore, these Miis all go out together on the same fishing excursion. They're eager to help the player catch a fish. Players can imagine how these Miis come from other parts of the world to theirs.

Good-Feel's *Battleground Z* (*StreetPass Zombies* in Europe and Japan, 2015) takes a different approach to its social mechanics. Other Miis/players aren't visitors; they're survivors. The game has a familiar zombie apocalypse scenario, and each level scatters Miis about. When the player saves them, they give the player a weapon based on the color of their clothes and run to safety. The player is the hero in this story, and having Miis to save reinforces this role, as it provides the player resources. As is the case with *Ultimate Angler*, having a variety of Miis wearing different colors gets the player different types of weapons. Certain weapons have strengths against different types of zombies.

Whenever possible, involving other players' characters directly in the story scenarios gives players added entertainment and much-needed resources. With friends' (or strangers'!) help, players progress through the game, but they also progress through the story.

conclusion

Whether the game is 2D or 3D or has no art assets at all, smart narrative design creates worlds that are believable and tangible for players. Traditional worldbuilding techniques, such as environmental narrative in level design, sounds, and background art, are all effective in mobile and social games. However, text and UI are just as effective, even when you *do* use more traditional techniques. In addition, if your game has social mechanics, this is an important element to make the world feel lived in. Friends' player characters can have natural roles in the world.

worldbuilding checklist

Figure out the world's major features. What is this world like? What is its history? What does the player need to know about it?

Know what kinds of assets you'll have to work with (and how many). Art, sound, and animation assets flesh out the world. If these are limited (or not used at all), you'll need to think of alternative means—like UI and text—to express the world to players.

Reuse assets when it makes sense to do so. An economy of assets keeps you within the project's scope and budget.

Show what you need to show, and suggest what you need to suggest. Players don't need to see and hear everything for the world to be believable. Use worldbuilding to engage players' imaginations.

when designing dynamic worlds

- Do your research!
- Consider whether the world needs cultures, magic/science/religion systems, etc. designed.
- Find believable worldbuilding explanations for the game's social mechanics.
  - What story scenario serves the reason why players send each other resources?
  - What story scenario serves the reason why players visit each other's cities, homes, resorts, etc.?
- Revise flavor text to illustrate aspects of the world to players.
- Incorporate worldbuilding into game modes.
  - Where in the world can these take place?
  - How do these modes relate to the world at large?

not just tutorial hosts
characters

Toiya Kristen Finley, PhD

contents

Characters provide us with someone to root for. They give us someone to root against. Well-written characters with developed personality flaws and strengths allow players to relate to them. We want to follow and participate in their journeys and wonder how they'll overcome all the conflicts the plot throws at them.

The makeup of good characters applies to characters of mobile and social games, just as they apply to characters of traditional games and other media. Well-written characters have strong characterization (i.e., the expression of the character's personality, motivations, and desires through dialogue and actions) and character development (the ways in which they change—for good or ill—throughout a story). Depending on the needs of the story, however, you may not write characters who are three-dimensional. The player may not interact with them much and may only see them once. That doesn't mean those characters can't leave an impression.

This chapter will look at some traditional and nontraditional techniques for the narrative design and writing of mobile game characters. First, let's look at characters in mobile/social games who have a role that's a little different than characters in traditional games.

Characters in mobile games and games on social networks can have a unique burden. Often, when you start a new game, you're greeted by a guide character with a specific responsibility that may determine the success of the game.

the guide character

App *onboarding* is a crucial step in maintaining users for any app. In essence, it's ensuring that users understand how to use an app right after they install it. If users *don't* understand the app after installing it, they're less likely to use it again.[*] From the perspective of mobile games, app onboarding is helping players understand as soon as possible how to play the game. The quicker they understand the gameplay, the quicker they can enjoy the experience. Player retention is crucial for the life of a mobile game. In 2015, 20%–40% of players returned to a game after a day-1 install.[†] If the game has a 30% second-day retention rate, this "is considered a huge success."[‡]

This is why *guide characters* have become a necessary part of social and mobile games. I'm using the term "guide character" to refer

---

[*] Megan Marrs, "App onboarding 101: 7 tips for creating engaged, informed users," *Localytics.com*, last modified April 27, 2016, http://info.localytics.com/blog/app-onboarding-101.

[†] Christopher Terwitte, "Engagement benchmarks deep-dive: A detailed look at games verticals," *Adjust.com*, last modified October 29, 2015, https://www.adjust.com/mobile-benchmarks-q3-2015/games-verticals/.

[‡] Tobias Heussner, Toiya Kristen Finley, Jennifer Brandes Hepler, and Ann Lemay, *The Game Narrative Toolbox* (Burlington, MA: Focal Press, 2015), 175.

to NPCs (nonplayer characters) in mobile and social games who show up immediately after players start the game and "guide" the player through tutorials. Guide characters do everything from explaining mechanics to showing players where to tap controls or access menus. Because of this, you need to write them a little differently when they first appear before the player.

Their dialogue must be concise and clear. While this is the case for all characters, it is especially true of guide characters. Remember, their responsibility is to *keep the player playing the game.* Yes, they're a bit of an instruction manual in this way, and the dialogue they speak may feel less natural or conversational. Their dialogue is usually accompanied by visuals and animated icons, such as blinking arrows pointing at buttons. For example, the tutorial helps the player build a house. The player needs tools. The button for the in-game shop glows white:

GUIDELY SWIPERIGHT: Hey there! Time to buy a hammer from the shop!

The guide character leaves no wiggle room for nuance and tells players exactly what they need to do.

You'll need to work closely with the game designer, artist, and UI/UX designer on the tutorial. *How* you present the instructions is just as important as what the guide character says. The guide character needs to work in tandem with the tutorial's visuals and sounds because these elements are just as important as any instructional text.

How the tutorial begins also deserves careful discussion. The tutorial should fit the game's genre and aesthetic. Therefore, a dress-up game will have a different pace and feel than an RPG. A more action-oriented game may place the beginning of the game in the midst of a battle and guide the player during the fight, while a tile-matching game may have more instructional dialogue up front to explain the mechanics.

After the tutorial gets players comfortable, guide characters, whenever possible, should have in-universe reasons for helping the player. Guide characters don't simply disappear once the tutorial's over. They're still a part of the game's world. By the very fact they've already helped players, guide characters have developed relationships with them. I've played several games where the guide character helps me through the tutorial, and then I've wondered, "Why do you want to help me? I've got nothing to do with you, and you've got nothing to do with me." Why are they so friendly? Perhaps I'm too suspicious, especially toward a fictional individual, but their helpfulness felt so *unnatural.*

Yes, they made me comfortable during the onboarding process—as they should. However, as those games progressed, I never got a sense of why those characters were invested in me, or if they had any lives of their own.

the team player and the voice of conscience: *dragonsoul* and *good knight story*

Guide characters created with in-universe motivations and perspectives not only are helpful to the player, but also have believable motivations for their involvement, which enhance their games' storytelling. *DragonSoul's* Unstable Understudy and *Good Knight Story's* leprechaun are two guide characters who have clear motivations for being invested in the player's success.

DragonSoul's (Fantasy Legend Studios/GREE, 2015) tutorial puts the player right into the conflict. As the game begins, the band of heroes battles against the villain Umlaut's minions. Unstable Understudy is one of the heroes with which the player begins the game. There isn't a player character (PC). Players don't have any in-game representations of themselves in the world. Players collect units (heroes) and choose up to five in each battle. However, in the way that Unstable Understudy addresses players, it's clear that she views them as a part of the team determined to defeat Umlaut. As this group travels the world in search of the evil dragon, the player journeys right along with them.

As Unstable Understudy instructs players on how to level up heroes, she keeps the focus on how it ultimately aids the fight against Umlaut. Screenshot from *DragonSoul*. © 2018 Fantasy Legend Studios, Inc. All rights reserved.

It makes sense, then, that Unstable Understudy wants to help the player understand the game. The player's success is directly tied to hers—and the fate of the world. Players unlock different game modes when they reach certain levels. Unstable Understudy remains in the guide-character role, introducing these game modes. She continues to treat the player as a member of the team. The Titan Temple features gigantic versions of several of the game's heroes. As the mode unlocks, Unstable Understudy confides in the player.

Unstable Understudy's relationship evolves beyond being a helpful guide. She sees the player as a trusted ally. Screenshot from *DragonSoul*. © 2018 Fantasy Legend Studios, Inc. All rights reserved.

Beyond her relationship with the player, however, she remains a main character in the story campaign. She has a definite role within the team of heroes, as well. A literal understudy, she's a student of the art of sorcery. The heroes often encounter strange magic or artifacts. Unstable Understudy is tasked to figure out their secrets. As guide characters tend to be, she's kind and helpful. If she gets into arguments with others during cutscenes, she's not mean-spirited. She serves as the story's narrator. In the Boss Pit mode, the three bosses have their own mini stories connected to the main one.

Unstable Understudy voices the plot during all three stages with each boss:

Screenshot from *DragonSoul.* © 2018 Fantasy Legend Studios, Inc. All rights reserved.

Unstable Understudy maintains her characterization through the tutorial and other modes where she serves as the helpful, friendly guide character. As the game and story progress, her motivations for aiding the player come into focus and remain consistent.

The leprechaun in *Good Knight Story* puts a spin on the guide character when it comes to his personality. *Good Knight Story* is a puzzle game with RPG elements. It has a fixed PC, a vain, disrespectful, and reckless knight. From his character portrait, the leprechaun looks like he's always ready to spar. He's sarcastic and mocks the knight. While this isn't typical behavior for a guide character, it fits *Good Knight Story's* overall aesthetic and story. The game's protagonist isn't a good guy. The leprechaun doesn't treat him like one, even though he helps him and tells him what to do as the knight advances through the story (and the player solves puzzles and advances through levels).

The leprechaun appears to be a figment of the knight's imagination. Therefore, he wants the knight to succeed because the knight's life is his life, too. So, it makes sense that he would tell the knight how to solve certain puzzles.

After the leprechaun's introduction, the knight wonders where the guide character came from. Screenshot from *Good Knight Story*. Developed/published by Turbo Chilli and is protected by United States and international copyright law. © Turbo Chilli

Players defeat NPCs by linking matching tiles for attacks. Combat is turn based. In this case, players can't defeat the ogre, but they need to remove the tiles to get to the four steins before the knight takes too much damage. Also, notice how the instructional dialogue uses the stein itself. Screenshot from *Good Knight Story*. Developed/published by Turbo Chilli and is protected by United States and international copyright law. © Turbo Chilli

While he's omniscient and knows how everything in the world works (read: how to play the game), the leprechaun is a part of both the knight's conscious and unconscious mind and serves as his conscience. At the beginning of the game, a brief cinematic shows the titular knight drinking in a raucous tavern with a group of knights. As gameplay begins, the knight wakes up, chained in a dungeon. He has no idea why he was jailed. He has no recollection at all. The leprechaun puts a twist on the amnesiac character.* While the knight can't remember anything, the leprechaun can pull up things from the knight's unconscious, things the knight has forgotten during his night of revelry, and explain why certain enemy NPCs want to challenge or kill him.

---

* Stories use the amnesiac PC trope to avoid lots of exposition. It would be unnatural if NPCs constantly told PCs things they should already know about themselves, for the player's benefit. Instead, because the PCs have amnesia, they learn things they've forgotten. The trope also is a technique used to aid player agency. Players and PCs learn together, building a connection between them. The trope has become a cliché. Serving as the knight's conscience, the leprechaun subverts this cliché.

As the story progresses, the knight develops a relationship with the leprechaun (again, somewhat unusual with guide characters). The leprechaun will even chide the knight for some of his behavior, suggesting that the knight is aware of his less than redeeming qualities.

The knight has a penchant for stealing vegetables. The leprechaun seems to think this is a problem. Apparently, the knight does, too. Screenshot from *Good Knight Story*. Developed/published by Turbo Chilli and is protected by United States and international copyright law. © Turbo Chilli

The knight's motivation for traveling the world and battling NPCs is to make amends for his actions the night before, which angered a dragon, put a princess's life in danger, and landed him in a dungeon. As the leprechaun occasionally shows up to give context to conflicts, he becomes the knight's traveling companion. Unlike Unstable Understudy, the leprechaun isn't directly involved with the game's plot, but he's an important companion for the knight... even if the knight is only talking to himself.

Developing guide characters beyond their onboarding roles will give players another source of entertainment. When writing them, consider the following to shape them into interesting characters:

- make sure their tutorial dialogue is clear and succinct and works in concert with the tutorial's visuals and sound design,
- keep their word choice in line with the game's overall tone,

- establish clear motivations for the guide character to help the player, and
- establish clear motivations and desires for their lives outside of assisting the player.

characterization and character development in mobile games

Traditionally, characters show their characterization and development through the game's story. The story includes quests and events in the story campaign, cinematics, and cutscenes.* While some mobile games use these storytelling techniques, you may find that other narrative tricks may be more appropriate. Whether you use conventional or unconventional means, characters still need to be interesting and entertaining. How you present them goes a long way to meeting that goal.

Good Knight Story (2016)

Good Knight Story's (Turbo Chilli) PC is arrogant and overconfident in his own skills. A compulsive risk taker, he's prone to gambling in situations that could get him killed. A wise guy, his mouth gets him into trouble, and he doesn't consider consequences. Unlike traditional knights, this PC doesn't have much of a moral code. He runs from responsibility, and he'll do anything to get out of a messy situation. All in all, the guy's kind of a jerk... and the "Good" in the game's title just might be ironic.

---

* Cinematics are in-game movies with no player interaction, while cutscenes are in-engine and may or may not include player interaction.

A couple of techniques illustrate the above characterization of *Good Knight Story*'s PC: (1) dialogue and (2) gameplay. Before fights begin, there's usually banter between the knight and the enemy NPC.

Screenshot from *Good Knight Story*. Developed/published by Turbo Chilli and is protected by United States and international copyright law. © Turbo Chilli

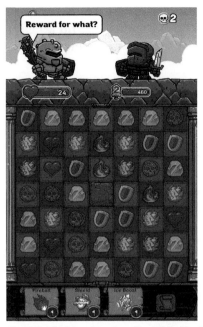

Screenshot from *Good Knight Story*. Developed/published by Turbo Chilli and is protected by United States and international copyright law. © Turbo Chilli

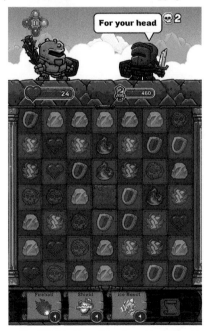

Screenshot from *Good Knight Story*. Developed/published by Turbo Chilli and is protected by United States and international copyright law. © Turbo Chilli

NPCs need lives too

Each NPC needs to have a relationship to the PC, even if it's to give a lore tidbit to explain something about the world. (This doesn't mean that NPCs shouldn't have lives that don't revolve around the PC, either.) For example, an NPC may only exist to say "Gregor's too tough to beat!" when players near a boss at the end of a level.

NPCs are a part of making the world feel believable and lived in. They shouldn't feel out of place for the world they inhabit. (And you would use your worldbuilding to design believable NPCs for that world.) NPCs support the PC via gameplay and/or story. They can be friends, allies, and fighting companions. They can provide feedback. They should have opinions about what the PC (and the player by extension) is doing in their world. They provide opportunities to explore the world though main quests and side quests. And enemies, mini bosses, and bosses provide players with conflicts and a way to progress through the story and the game.

Good Knight Story's enemy NPCs have their own clear motivations and desires. When NPCs are simply obstacles to destroy, the world and the game can feel one note. Players may not mind this, but the gameplay experience becomes more interesting when the enemies are not just there to be slaughtered. An enemy that taunts the PC (and the player by extension) gives the player even more motivation to beat it. In the case of a PC who sits in a morally gray area (or is simply a plain awful individual), players might feel torn that they have to beat a "good" NPC, in that cringe-inducing "I don't wanna, but I have to!" way. Several of the NPCs in *Good Knight Story* have significant beefs with the PC. Their motivations for wanting to kill the knight reveal their own desires and personalities.

Screenshot from *Good Knight Story*. Developed/published by Turbo Chilli and is protected by United States and international copyright law. © Turbo Chilli

Screenshot from *Good Knight Story*. Developed/published by Turbo Chilli and is protected by United States and international copyright law. © Turbo Chilli

Interactions with NPCs also help to characterize PCs. That knight... what a swell guy! Screenshot from *Good Knight Story*. Developed/published by Turbo Chilli and is protected by United States and international copyright law. © Turbo Chilli

NPCs can give more characterization to a PC, as well. How they perceive a PC gives the player more information about the PC. After all, people don't always see themselves clearly. The same should be true for believable characters. While NPCs can be biased for or against a PC, there can be truth to what they say.

The knight encounters NPCs who wish to avenge a dead loved one, fight for their honor once the knight insults them, and defeat the knight to claim the bounty on his head. While those are simple motivations, other interactions reveal that some NPCs are morally complex. It's the knight's fault the princess has been kidnapped by a normally peaceful dragon. The PC makes a deal with the king: either the knight rescues the princess, or the dragon kills him. Either way, that's a win-win for the king.

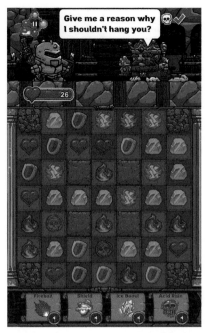

Screenshot from *Good Knight Story*. Developed/published by Turbo Chilli and is protected by United States and international copyright law. © Turbo Chilli

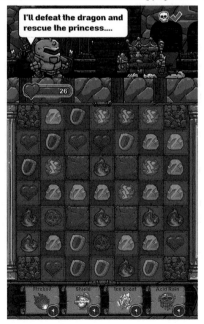

Screenshot from *Good Knight Story*. Developed/published by Turbo Chilli and is protected by United States and international copyright law. © Turbo Chilli

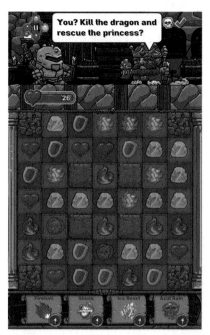

Screenshot from *Good Knight Story*. Developed/published by Turbo Chilli and is protected by United States and international copyright law. © Turbo Chilli

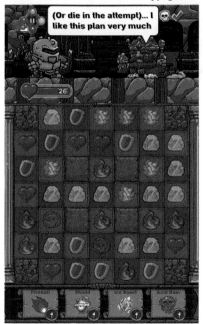

The king can't lose. Screenshot from *Good Knight Story*. Developed/published by Turbo Chilli and is protected by United States and international copyright law. © Turbo Chilli

Good Knight Story's traditional branching dialogue

While the knight is a fixed character, players do get some choice in expressing who he is through dialogue. Branching dialogue is a traditional technique in developing stories and characters in games. In *Good Knight Story*, it acts much in the same way. The knight speaks with barkeeps when he reaches taverns on the map. Here, players get to choose how the knight comes across. They can have him lie or own up to his behavior. They can have him be a jerk... or less of a jerk.

Screenshot from *Good Knight Story*. Developed/published by Turbo Chilli and is protected by United States and international copyright law. © Turbo Chilli

This time the knight's likely telling the truth when he says he doesn't know this barkeep, but based on who the knight is, this doesn't mean the barkeep believes him. Screenshot from *Good Knight Story*. Developed/published by Turbo Chilli and is protected by United States and international copyright law. © Turbo Chilli

With branching dialogue, the PC still needs to remain in character, even when there are a couple or more options.

Screenshot from *Good Knight Story*. Developed/published by Turbo Chilli and is protected by United States and international copyright law. © Turbo Chilli

Screenshot from *Good Knight Story*. Developed/published by Turbo Chilli and is protected by United States and international copyright law. © Turbo Chilli

The knight didn't pay his tab... *Shocking.* Screenshot from *Good Knight Story*. Developed/published by Turbo Chilli and is protected by United States and international copyright law. © Turbo Chilli

Good Knight Story's branching dialogue serves a few purposes. It gives the player clues as to what the knight has done, and players can return to these conversations to get more information. (The screenshots from The Loading Bar show alternate choices for dialogue with the barkeep.) Sometimes the dialogue serves as an intro to a battle inside the tavern, as is the case where the leprechaun tells the knight about his bet with the barkeep. Additionally, a dialogue choice will net players some gold. It comes as a nice surprise.

A lot of mobile games don't have branching dialogue trees. However, they make sense in *Good Knight Story* because the game is an RPG.

For all of *Good Knight Story's* dialogue, the key here is that these are *brief* interactions, key for short play sessions. Players don't have a lot of time to read through long conversations. Dialogue between the knight and enemies appears in small speech bubbles that are quickly digestible. The lines of dialogue are short sentences and phrases, and exchanges are usually not more than three lines between characters. Even the branching dialogue in the taverns tends to be about four lines each between the knight and barkeep.

characterization through nonstory means: *dragonsoul*

I detail the ways *DragonSoul* expresses worldbuilding through its game modes and features in Chapter 3. It uses similar techniques for its characterization and character development. As is the case with its worldbuilding, *DragonSoul* takes every opportunity to inform players about its characters through nontraditional storytelling and story delivery.

DragonSoul's narrative design influences character skills, animations, and art.

Characterization through Flavor Text

We know that text is one of the traditional ways we tell stories and provide descriptions that engage player imaginations. In Chapter 3, I discuss how lore and flavor text flesh out the world. You can apply lore and flavor text in similar ways to illustrate characters' personalities, what's important to them, and maybe even some trivia about them. All of *DragonSoul's* characters have unique skills based upon their character types.

Dragon Lady is dour with an acerbic wit. Her skills are based on insults and include descriptive names like "Flippant Missile," "Backhander," and "Attack of Ridicule." The names themselves are important and a part of her characterization. They all describe something about her personality.

Screenshot from *DragonSoul.* © 2018 Fantasy Legend Studios, Inc. All rights reserved.

Dragon Lady's flippant, she gives backhanded compliments, and she ridicules others. Also, each of these skills has some flavor text mixed in to explain their function and attributes. The description for "Backhander" begins "Slaps a random foe with a backhanded compliment...."

She seems nice.... Screenshot from *DragonSoul*. © 2018 Fantasy Legend Studios, Inc. All rights reserved.

DragonSoul's flavor text also gives players a sense of the heroes' community, as it takes opportunities to express character relationships and interactions. An earlier version of Aquatic Man's stats suggests that he has hero friends over and entertains them, but one of them has a nasty habit.

Screenshot from *DragonSoul*. © 2018 Fantasy Legend Studios, Inc. All rights reserved.

So, any flavor text you write can describe a character, connect that character to others and express their relationships and interactions, and express how that character fits in with the game's wider world. *DragonSoul* even uses character-centric flavor text for the skins players can choose for each hero. Again, flavor text and lore are versatile. You can use them whether a game is story-oriented or has little or no story.

The Stories of Legendary Skills

While skills characterize *DragonSoul's* heroes, unlocking legendary skills is the primary means in which heroes receive development. Legendary skills take time to unlock, and players do so through quest chains occurring in three stages. What players must do to complete quests vary.

For the first stage of Orc Monk's quest, players must pay $5,000,00 in gold. Screenshots from *DragonSoul.* © 2018 Fantasy Legend Studios, Inc. All rights reserved.

You might wonder why I'm including something like quests under "nonstory means." While quests often tell a story, they're used in *DragonSoul* as an RPG element to improve heroes. Oftentimes in RPGs, players can unlock new skills or level up characters just through the gameplay itself. In *DragonSoul*, there are both hero levels and skill levels. Hero levels correspond to the player's overall level. So, if the player is level 110, they can raise a hero's level from 108 to 110. However, players don't unlock skills based on their overall or hero levels. Players promote heroes (based on color scheme) to reach a new skill tier. To promote heroes, players need to loot six kinds of gear for each promotion level. This takes a lot of grinding, as different kinds of scraps and scrolls in specific quantities can make up a piece of gear.

However, grinding loot and leveling up heroes—traditional ways to level up skills—is only part of unlocking legendary skills. Players must promote heroes to orange to unlock the legendary quests. Adding the story element improves upon the gameplay experiences of grinding through the quest chain's three stages. (Read more about structuring quests in Chapter 6, "I Seek the Grail (in Five Minutes or Less): Designing and Writing Quests for Mobile Games.")

Each quest has a story with a well-defined plot, told in three parts, one part per stage. The quest usually includes at least one other hero. This allows the game to tell players about those other characters and how they're interacting in the community of heroes and their wider world. Part one (stage one) introduces the hero's conflict. The conflict can be anything from wanting to grow stronger as a hero, improving on a hobby, or trying out new music.

Bone Dragon, a loner, tries hanging out with other heroes and listening to the music they enjoy. Screenshots from *DragonSoul*. © 2018 Fantasy Legend Studios, Inc. All rights reserved.

Each stage includes a beginning and ending cutscene using dialogue text boxes and character portraits. As the player completes stage three, the story concludes with the character gaining some new insight about himself or herself. Again, these may or may not be grand epiphanies, but the characters have changed in some way, even if their experiences have made them more stubborn and solidified their beliefs.

(*Continued*)

(**Continued**) Rabid Dragon's entire quest chain, which shows off both Rabid Dragon's and Groovy Druid's personalities and interests. Notice how it uses the Titan Temple game mode, and Groovy Druid references it as a location in the world (effective worldbuilding). Screenshots from *DragonSoul*. © 2018 Fantasy Legend Studios, Inc. All rights reserved.

If it's within your game's scope, think of how you can add similar story scenarios to quests that unlock your game's features.

Animations

If your game has animations, you can communicate things about those characters in the way they move. Injured characters hunch over and drag their sides. Dangerous characters players need to avoid might lurch before they take off into an all-out sprint in pursuit. Animations can also express who characters are, what's important to them, and what motivates them.

In *DragonSoul*, every hero has unique animations that reflect their personalities and interests. Animations are for their skills, winning animations, and death animations. Let's look at Dragon Lady's Attack of Ridicule. The one-line description begins, "Slaps everyone in front of her... ." The skill's animation shows exactly that.

Attack of Ridicule's animation is a giant, slapping handprint that snaps on the screen. Screenshot from *DragonSoul*. © 2018 Fantasy Legend Studios, Inc. All rights reserved.

Here, *DragonSoul* uses the maxim "Play, don't tell." Players see what they've read about their heroes in action. Their personalities are on full display in their behavior. For players who *don't* read the flavor text for skill descriptions, they can still get an accurate sense of each character from watching their animations.

Bardbarian shreds her guitar as she powers up. Her axe (guitar) is also her axe (weapon). Screenshot from *DragonSoul.* © 2018 Fantasy Legend Studios, Inc. All rights reserved.

Orc Monk ascends to the heavens as he dies. Screenshot from *DragonSoul.* © 2018 Fantasy Legend Studios, Inc. All rights reserved.

Polemaster, who's skilled at, um, pole mastering, does a literal death drop when he dies. Screenshot from *DragonSoul.* © 2018 Fantasy Legend Studios, Inc. All rights reserved.

N. B. *DragonSoul* animates skills, which reflect hero personalities. However, whether a game has animations or not, you can use skills in characterizing characters. Just a line of text explaining a skill or ability can say a lot about the character. Also, if the game doesn't have animations but does use character portraits, you can convey characters' personalities through their various poses. When you write up character bios or sheets, include a section that talks about the character's personality and demeanor. (If creating characters and/or writing their bios isn't one of your tasks, you can still discuss characterizing them through art and animation with the game designer and creative lead.) Give descriptions of the character's physicality, posture, etc. to give artists ideas of how aspects of their personality and attitude come through in their physicality.

The leprechaun in *Good Knight Story* always has his fists raised, as if he's scrappy and waiting for a fight. His posture reflects his attitude and is a reflection on the knight, as well.

What do animations say about your characters?

- Is their personality reflected in the way they move/walk?
- Do they have skills or abilities that reflect their personalities?
- Can their animations express their current physical condition (injured, powered up, etc.)?

conclusion

Depending on your game's needs, you can use traditional storytelling, nontraditional storytelling, or both. While mobile games may not have the capacity for cinematics, cutscenes, and extensive dialogue trees, their limitations give narrative designers and writers plenty of innovative opportunities for characterization and character development.

characters checklist

Who is the game's guide character? The guide character needs to support players and aid in making the onboarding process as smooth as possible. The tone of the guide character's dialogue needs to match the overall tone of the game.

Give NPCs believable motivations. All NPCs (even minor, one-dimensional ones) should have clear roles in the story.

Use flavor text and/or lore. Both flavor text and lore can express characterization and reveal the nature of relationships between characters.

Incorporate characterizations into animation and art. If they're within the game's scope, character animation and art provide strong behaviors and visuals to illustrate character personalities.

as you're revising...

- Make sure the guide character's tutorial dialogue is succinct, is working in concert with tutorial visuals and instructional texts, and is easy to follow.
- Rework lines of dialogue to better reflect each character's personality.
- Think of names for character skills and attributes that illustrate who those characters are. Add flavor text to those skills and attributes.
- Write descriptions for animators, artists, and sound designers into character bios that will give them a sense of the characters' personalities, demeanors, behaviors, etc.

more than pretty words
functional dialogue

Toiya Kristen Finley, PhD

contents

Dialogue is an important component of storytelling. It's an easy way to express character development and characterization, and to move plots forward and foreshadow events or character fates. When discussing dialogue, writers usually do this from a *creative writing* perspective. Even narrative designers and game writers tend to focus on dialogue's place in a game's story. It's one of the most common ways player characters and NPCs interact, and it is a major aspect of traditional stories in games. However, there's also the *narrative design* of dialogue. Dialogue in games is more than just a story vehicle. Dialogue's narrative design is, arguably, more important than its role in the story.

In other words, how are the game design and gameplay reflected and represented in the dialogue? How is the dialogue part of the gameplay? It must communicate tutorial instructions, mechanics, and mission objectives and updates, among other gameplay elements. Before writing any dialogue, it's always good to ask, "What is its function?"

Because dialogue should be *strategic.*

No matter the storytelling medium, every line of dialogue should have a specific reason (or reasons) to be there. Even in long conversation trees with NPCs, each line of dialogue has a specific function. In other words, it has something specific to communicate to players.

dialogue's purpose in games

Dialogue has several functions in videogames. We can divide these into aspects of narrative design and game writing. The game may present dialogue in a number of formats. A character may speak it directly to the player, it may be in a notification, it can appear in a menu, or it may appear in other in-game descriptions.

NARRATIVE DESIGN'S DIALOGUE FUNCTIONS

- *Guide players through a tutorial*: At the beginning of a game (and at specific points), a character explains controls, skills, abilities, etc. to players and tells them why these mechanics and controls are important.
- *Give mission objectives*: A character tells players exactly what they need to do to successfully complete a mission or quest.

- *Introduce a new mechanic*: The game teaches players a new mechanic and how it works.
- *Explain a new skill*: The game teaches players a new skill and how it works.

GAME WRITING'S DIALOGUE FUNCTIONS

- *Give background/lore*: Characters may say something about past events or give worldbuilding insights.
- *Convey character development*: Speaking characters, including the player character, may express their own character development, or characters may indicate they've noticed changes in a specific character.
- *Express characterization*: How characters speak (their accents/verbal tics, whether they use slang or "hifalutin" language, their diction), and what they choose to talk about illustrate aspects of the characters' personalities and what's important to them.
- *Introduce a plot point/foreshadow future plot points*: Characters may drop a subtle or not-so-subtle hint about something that happens later.

For less story-oriented games, dialogue's narrative design will be more applicable. For more story-oriented and character-oriented games, *all* of these aspects falling under narrative design and game writing apply. But the functional dialogue in a game more focused on gameplay should still be story-oriented while serving its purpose—dialogue should *always* reflect its speaker's personality.

Clever writing can make the narrative design functions of dialogue seem less... functional. In Chapter 4, I talked about the importance of guide characters and why their dialogue needs to be easy to follow. However, dialogue giving instructions/information can sound rote, technical, and out of place if it's not grounded in the voice of the character speaking it or the world in which it exists:

GUIDELY SWIPERIGHT: Hey there! Look at that menu to the right of the screen.

GUIDELY SWIPERIGHT (cont'd): Click on it.

GUIDELY SWIPERIGHT (cont'd): That's your inventory!

Sure, players are used to getting information via characters this way. There's nothing wrong with it, per se. But it *can* momentarily take players out of the world, and characters speaking these lines seem a little less natural. If there's a chance to make this dialogue feel more natural, to feel more blended into the world of the game, why not take it?

What if good ol' Guidely was the captain's mate on a pirate ship? This is how he might speak:

GUIDELY SWIPERIGHT: Ahoy there! Look at that menu to the right of the screen, matey!

GUIDELY SWIPERIGHT (cont'd): Click on it.

GUIDELY SWIPERIGHT (cont'd): Aye, that's your inventory!

Five Nights at Freddy's Phone Guy: Totally Untrustworthy (But Not When It Comes to Gameplay Instructions)

Phone Guy, *Five Nights at Freddy's* deuteragonist, is memorable to the franchise's fans. Even though he works at a pizza place with murderous animatronics, he has a nonchalant personality. In fact, he seems to be *okay* with working in such an environment. The player is a nighttime security guard, and Phone Guy takes it upon himself to get the new guard acclimated via phone messages. The first two nights, Phone Guy talks about what the job entails, which is basically the game's tutorial.

Phone Guy's "Night 2" dialogue introduces game mechanics:

Uh… interestingly enough, Freddy himself doesn't come off stage very often. I heard he becomes a lot more active in the dark though, so, hey, I guess that's one more reason not to run out of power, right? I-I also want to emphasize the importance of using your door lights. There are blind spots in your camera views, and those blind spots happen to be right outside of your doors. So if-if you can't find something, or someone, on your cameras, be sure to check the door lights. Uh, you might only have a few seconds to react…. Uh, not that you would be in any danger, of course. I'm not implying that.*

---

* "*Five Nights at Freddy's 1* Phone Calls." *Genius.com*, accessed August 10, 2017, https://genius.com/Phone-guy-five-nights-at-freddys-1-phone-calls-annotated.

In the game, the player remains stationary in an office, unable to get up from the seat. Two open doors lead inside of the office on either side. Four animatronics lurk around at night, trying to make their way into the office to kill the security guard. The only defenses the player has are the lights outside the door to see when something—*someone*—approaches, the ability to shut the doors on either side of the office, and battery life to turn on the lights and shut the doors to keep the animatronics out. During "Night 1," Phone Guy explains the job and a little about the setting and the animatronics. This allows players to play around with the controls and get used to the environment. The "Night 2" level is when animatronics start roaming, and players have to defend themselves. Phone Guy's functional dialogue reflects this.

Guide players through a tutorial:

- Phone Guy explicitly tells players about an animatronic's behaviors and how to look out for it: "... Freddy himself doesn't come off stage very often. I heard he becomes a lot more active in the dark though."
- Animatronics can strike quickly. Players had better stay alert and on guard: "Uh, you might only have a few seconds to react."

Introduce a new mechanic:

- Battery power is extremely important to control closing the doors and keeping the animatronics outside of the office. Players will need to preserve it as much as possible: "... I guess that's one more reason not to run out of power, right?"
- Using the door lights can alert players to what critter is lurking outside the office: "I-I also want to emphasize the importance of using your door lights. There are blind spots in your camera views, and those blind spots happen to be right outside of your doors. So if-if you can't find something, or someone, on your cameras, be sure to check the door lights."

Explain a new skill:

- Players get used to the game space in "Night 1." There's really no danger as they learn to use the controls, and Phone Guy tells them about the job and their nighttime

~~hell-beast~~ companions. The "Night 2" dialogue explains the controls and mechanics and why they're necessary for the player's survival.

All of this information is conversational. Each line of dialogue, and the instructions themselves, are grounded in Phone Guy's personality and the world of *Five Nights at Freddy's*, pointing to the dialogue's game-writing characteristics.

Express characterization:
- Phone Guy has several verbal tics to illustrate his personality. He hesitates and stutters ("Uh...," "I-I...," "... if-if...").
- He hints that something sinister is going on, but he's nonchalant about it. This signals that he might not be all that trustworthy: "Uh, you might only have a few seconds to react.... Uh, not that you would be in any danger, of course. I'm not implying that."

Introduce a plot point/foreshadow future plot points:
- "Night 1" foreshadows the danger to come: "Uh, let's see. First there's an introductory greeting from the company that I'm supposed to read. Uh, it's kind of a legal thing, you know.... Upon discovering that damage or death has occurred, a missing person report will be filed within 90 days, or as soon [as] property and premises have been thoroughly cleaned and bleached, and the carpets have been replaced."*

The dialogue clearly tells players how to play, but it feels like a natural part of the world and grounded in Phone Guy's personality. You can apply any of these narrative-design or game-writing techniques to dialogue in mobile games.

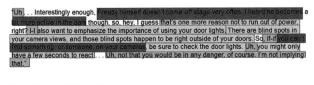

You can weave together lines of dialogue with different functions so that they sound natural.

---

* "*Five Nights at Freddy's 1* Phone Calls," *Genius.com*, accessed August 10, 2017. https://genius.com/Phone-guy-five-nights-at-freddys-1-phone-calls-annotated.

dialogue challenges in mobile games

But technical and budget constraints can limit what you can do with dialogue as a narrative designer or game writer. In many games, players won't see their avatar or the player character speaking to NPCs in the environment. Most likely, you won't have voiced dialogue or dialogue choices. You'll be writing fewer, shorter lines of dialogue, unless you're working on a text-based game. However, as is true with other constraints, these limitations present opportunities. You can get creative with what you do with dialogue and how players will engage with that dialogue as a result.

Write for the Smartphone Screen

Tablets provide bigger screens for larger text boxes and longer lines of dialogue, but plan to write for the smartphone screen instead.* Plenty of players will play games on their tablets, but you have to account for all of the other players who'll be accessing games on their smartphones. Lines of dialogue need to be shorter, while still being straightforward, being easy to understand, and containing all of their functional information. Longer lines of dialogue may end up cut off on the smartphone screen, which forces players to scroll through lines.

A good way to practice more succinct dialogue is using Twitter. Limit yourself to 140 characters, and think about what you're trying to say and how the tone will come across. Force yourself to stick to those 140 characters without using abbreviations, dropping vowels from words to make them shorter, or (*ahem*) writing ungrammatically.

Part of this is a UI issue. How big (or small) will the dialogue text boxes be? How many characters (not words!) can you fit in a dialogue text box or on one line? The developers or studio working on the project may already have these limitations figured out. Character limitations are one of the first things you want to ask about if you're tasked with writing dialogue or UI content. However, I've been on several projects where the developers hadn't considered how much text should appear on the screen at one time. If you find yourself in this situation, it's good to have a conversation with the leads (creative director, producer, game designer, UI designer) to determine what the right limitations should be.

---

* Keep in mind that—even when you are writing for smartphone screens—there are a range of screen sizes.

Something else to keep in mind: you don't want to force players to scroll (or tap) through dialogue. Many players like to skip dialogue. Forcing them to scroll can leave them frustrated. This especially will be a problem if that dialogue contains important gameplay information/ instructions. The more lines of dialogue on the screen at one time, the more likely they're not all going to fit. It's better to have only one or two lines at a time. Players may have to tap, but they won't have to read incomplete, cutoff lines. The maximum number of lines on the screen at one time is something else you can discuss with the team.

Handling Conversations in 2D

If characters will engage in conversations, you'll also have to think about how to present these in-game. Unlike PC or console games, players may not be interacting with NPCs in the environment. They can't walk up to them and start a conversation. Also, it's common in mobile and social games for characters to have conversations without the player avatar's involvement.* The traditional way to handle this in mobile and social games is to place character portraits with accompanying text boxes on the screen. Depending on the character portrait and text box sizes, you can fit up to four characters on the screen at once. As one character speaks, its text box and portrait light up. The other characters on the screen are greyed out. This directs the player's eye to the character currently speaking. Another benefit of presenting dialogue this way is that previous lines of dialogue remain on the screen. Players can read anything they missed or didn't understand.

---

* This often happens in cutscenes or games where players have several "units," hero characters they collect, as in *DragonSoul*.

DragonSoul's solution to having multiple speakers on the screen at once. Notice how the dialogue is based on the personality of each hero. Screenshot from *DragonSoul.* © 2018 Fantasy Legend Studios, Inc. All rights reserved.

A trope from visual novels is to place character portraits on the screen with the corresponding dialogue text boxes underneath. This can work well for limited screen space. *Mystery Match* uses a variation of this. Instead of two character portraits, there's always one character speaking at a time with the dialogue text box under the character portrait. There's flexibility with the character portraits themselves and the emotional states they convey.

Screenshot from *Mystery Match*. Developed/published by Outplay Entertainment and protected by United States and international copyright law. © Outplay Entertainment

Two of Emma's emotional states. (Screenshots are from an older version of the game.) Screenshot from *Mystery Match*. Developed/published by Outplay Entertainment and protected by United States and international copyright law. © Outplay Entertainment

Voiced Dialogue vs. Text-Based Dialogue

Most mobile games will not have voiced dialogue. Because a voice actor reads the lines, you don't want to make lines of dialogue difficult to read. While you may use these in moderation, when you write lines stringing together assonance,* consonance,† alliteration,‡

---

* The repetition of the same vowel sounds in adjacent words starting with different consonants: "The rain in Spain... ."
† The repetition of consonant sounds: "Keeping perfect pitch takes discipline."
‡ The repetition of consonant sounds at the beginning of a series of words: "Stop sticking steaks on the steel stove."

and verbal/vocal tics,* and use flowery/ornate language,† these can trip up the actor's tongue and sound unnatural to the player. Eye dialect‡ can make the character sound too caricaturish or uneducated, even if the writing is an accurate phonetic representation of the accent.

Also, the benefit of voice actors is that they can express the characters' personalities through accents (therefore, no need for eye dialect) and inflections to express how grandiose or silly a character comes across (cutting down the need for stylistic choices like assonance, consonance, and lots of flowery language).

And while you might include a sprinkling of made-up words here and there from lore, you'll also want to avoid overdoing it. This can sound preposterous and garbled, and it can confuse players who can't put all of those made-up words into context.

However, alliteration, assonance, consonance, flowery language, and preposterous-sounding lore work in *text-based* dialogue. These make the writing more interesting and amusing, and they work with the overall tone of the story. This kind of language helps the overall atmosphere. Over-the-top language is especially good when the game or the character is over the top. And since there's no voice actor to express the character's personality, accent, and verbal tics, the writing needs to do this. A word or two written in eye dialect help players "hear" pronunciation, but you don't want to overdo it in text-based dialogue, either. It can be a slog to read.

text *IS* visual

"Show, don't tell" is a popular axiom in writing (as it should be), but what we can easily forget is that text can also show *because* it's visual. There are a lot of things we can imply by the way text looks.

Thi*s* **font'***s* personality is different than this font's and *this font's.*

---

* A vocalization or word an individual utters with frequency (sometimes to show nerves or anxiety). *The Lord of the Rings's* Gollum has several verbal tics, including "precious."

† Any combination of assonance, consonance, alliteration, made-up words, etc.: "The gauche and grotesque Manrey has the *audacity* to bribe the majestic magistrate of Blytheheight!"

‡ Misspellings to phonetically represent accents and dialect: "Heya! Watcha doin'?"

You can develop a visual style in a mobile game, and players will quickly figure out that when characters speak words in red, they're angry; when the text box has icicles hanging off of it, the character is being emotionally cold toward the addressee; etc. You can use text to convey a lot of things.

WHAT TEXT CONVEYS

Characteristics and personalities: What characters say (word choice) reveals their characterization. A character who greets you with "How ya doin'?" would probably not say, "Well, hello there, my dear."

Accents/dialects: Some words spelled phonetically to mimic an accent or dialect can tell players where that character is from.

Mood: The way in which you present words can tell players about a character's mood or physical state: "I'm so *tiiirrrrred*" or "I'd suggest you NOT talk to me right now!"

Sarcasm: Italics or all caps, in context, make a character come across as sarcastic: "Oh, how *thoughtful* of you! I never would have figured it out myself."

Location: Characters can suggest where they are in the world in relation to the player/player character. (See the *Fat Chicken* analysis later in this chapter.)

Onomatopoeia: Onomatopoetic words convey nonverbalizations:

sigh

GAG

Tee hee!

Emphasis: All caps, bolding, and italics suggest where characters are placing *emphasis* as they speak, whether they're SHOUTING or RAISING THEIR VOICES or **highlighting** something.

When you're working with the team (or if the team is you), talk about the fonts you're going to use, and discuss how you want to convey textual tricks (like emphasis or onomatopoeia). Some font sets may not include bold or italics.

Think about all of the ways you might express characters' personalities and emotional states through the *visuals* of text.

Design for Dialogue Text Boxes

While the user interface artist, art director, producer, and lead game designer will determine the look of the game's text boxes, you can make suggestions as the narrative designer. Text boxes aid in communicating tone, personality, and whether a character is thinking or speaking. Thanks to a history of comics and manga, text boxes already have an established visual language from speech balloons. You can use the knowledge players already have from comics and manga to your advantage.

THE SHAPE OF DIALOGUE BALLOONS

Shapes of dialogue balloons convey how a character says a line:

Jagged: Screaming or shouting

Icy (with hanging icicles): Hostility toward the addressee

Rough: Monstrous, sinister (good for creatures, too)

Electronic: Robotic or indicating transmission over electronic devices

Wavy: Drunk or high

Discuss with your team whether designing different shapes for dialogue text boxes would be practical. These shapes are advantageous if the game has no voiced dialogue, and you give players visuals to suggest tone, personality, attitude, etc. along with words. An added benefit of text box shapes is that they help players who are hearing impaired, if the games have voiced dialogue or emotes/onomatopes. Players can see the shape of the text box and imagine how the character sounds.

fat chicken: Gravy and Ms. Melendez

I worked on Relevant Games's *Fat Chicken* (2014), a reverse tower defense that takes a satirical look at factory farming. While the game is light on story, the developer wanted to address the dangers of factory farming through two NPCs: one representing an anti-factory-farming stance, and the other taking a pro-factory-farming stance. Players work at the Fat Chicken Meat Company™. Each level, they fatten up animals and then collect their meat. They begin as a janitor and chicken feeder, and work their way to the top of the executive ladder to become the CEO. The game's story progresses after every few levels, where the NPCs will talk to them about improving Fat Chicken's profits, discuss the environmental problems the company is creating in the game's world, or try to dissuade players from continuing factory farming.

Gravy and Location

The anti-stance guy, Barry "Gravy" Graveson, has been a proponent of ending factory farming for a while and heads a group that's trying to take down Fat Chicken. Their activities include attempting to sabotage Fat Chicken's local farms across the United States. During the first level, Gravy recognizes that the player has taken an entry level job at Fat Chicken. He hides at a factory farm and tries to recruit the player to his side.

Fat Chicken's design does not include a player-character avatar interacting directly with NPCs. A player character does not appear anywhere in-game. The NPCs speak to the player via text boxes designed to include their character portraits and dialogue. Since players can't see Gravy hiding and trying to get their attention, I had to convey this solely through dialogue.

Screenshot from *Fat Chicken*. Developed/published by Relevant Games and is protected by United States and international copyright law. © Relevant Games

To show that Gravy isn't near the character, I use onomatopoeia: "Psst.... " Gravy then says, "... over here, dude" to signal to players that this new character isn't in a face-to-face conversation (a default assumption when a character portrait is directly in front of a player), nor is he physically near them. Players have to imagine themselves making their way over to *him*. "Psst" also suggests someone wants to keep things quiet or tell a secret. Through the line of dialogue, "Psst, over here, dude," I'm letting players know that Gravy isn't near them, he wants to get their attention, and he's probably trying to hide something.

At the same time, the lines have game-writing functions. Gravy's laidback and hippyish. I use both the character portrait and dialogue to show this to players. His pronunciation is lax: "Sher" instead of "Sure." Players can hear his lack of enunciation and marry it to his hippy image.

Melendez and Visual Verbal Tics

Ms. Melendez is the game's guide character* and Fat Chicken's HR manager. She leads players through the tutorial and represents Fat Chicken's pro-factory-farming stance throughout the game's story. No nonsense, blunt, and dedicated to the corporation, Melendez' goal is to make Fat Chicken as profitable as it can be. She keeps that goal as the players' primary focus, whether she's giving them a new objective or participating in the newest plot point.

Since Melendez is loyal to the corporation and concerned with profits, this gave me the opportunity to play around with her dialogue's visuals. These are "visual verbal tics," so to speak. Words associated with money or financial gains I spelled with an American dollar sign standing in for "s" and the American cent sign standing in for "c." Also, because she is so dedicated to Fat Chicken and is well versed in corporate speak, she often says the company's name in full, which is followed by the trademark symbol, or company branding and marketing slogans. When she introduces herself to players, she says "Fat Chicken Meat Company™," the company's philosophy for its employees ("The Fat Chicken Way™"), and "su¢¢e$$."

---

* For more on the role of guide characters, see Chapter 4, "Not Just Tutorial Hosts: Characters."

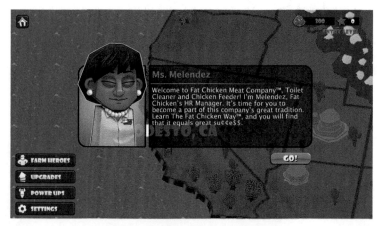

Screenshot from *Fat Chicken*. Developed/published by Relevant Games and is protected by United States and international copyright law. © Relevant Games

A hallmark we can aim for in writing good dialogue is that the reader or player can figure out who's speaking the dialogue without hearing that character's voice or seeing a corresponding image. *Fat Chicken's* lead designer, Randy Greenback, wrote the tutorial and informational texts, but I tweaked some of these lines so that they read in Melendez' voice.* These texts don't have her portrait in the text box, but players can still "hear" her because they're written in her personality and use her visual verbal tics:

---

* If someone other than the narrative designer/game writer is responsible for writing instructional and/or informational texts, you can ask the writer to revise these lines so that they're in a character's voice.

Screenshot from *Fat Chicken*. Developed/published by Relevant Games and is protected by United States and international copyright law. © Relevant Games

Use visual verbal tics sparingly, as is the case with eye dialect. It can be difficult and frustrating reading lots of symbols and other visual cues. They can become unintelligible or undecipherable. (Think about how you might have to decode "l33t speak" or a Twitter or text message with the vowels dropped, and you'll get a good idea of how players have to figure out a line of dialogue.) Most players won't have the patience for them and will likely skip them, a problem if they contain important information. The other problem with an overuse of visual verbal tics is that they lose their effectiveness. Players might gloss over them or ignore them all together.

Fat Chicken's Emotional States

Different portraits for emotional states also enhance dialogue. You don't need a lot of these; a basic range will do. But an image expressing a particular emotion can help the player "hear" the character's emotion. You can discuss with your lead and art team how many emotional states you can include in the game, according to your budget and technical constraints. When you write your dialogue, you can pair the lines with an emotional state, so the coders know which portraits to include:

GRAVY (Happy): I'm with the WWW. Sher you've heard of us.
PC: [Unspoken dialogue.]
GRAVY (Flustered): No, not like "World Wide Web."

Gravy's introduction includes four of his emotional states to help make his conversation with the player character more dynamic. He reacts emotionally in words and image.

Gravy knows he needs to peace out, or else. Screenshot from *Fat Chicken*. Developed/published by Relevant Games and is protected by United States and international copyright law.
© Relevant Games

You can suggest to players an NPC's emotions without using animation.

The One-Sided Conversation

I want to make a note about Gravy's conversation above. The story is linear, and the player character is fixed. The player character in *Fat Chicken* has very specific motives, starting with wanting to be great at a new job after being out of work for so long. There's no branching narrative, and the player character ascends the company's corporate ladder. In other words, since the PC is fixed, the player's not making choices as to whom the player character is going to be or what the player character is going to say in any conversation. Gravy responds to the PC's unspoken questions and answers. The player character makes an assumption about what "WWW" stands for and turns down Gravy's invitation to fight against Fat Chicken. Because the PC is fixed and the player does not have any influence on the story, the player character can make these unspoken responses to which Gravy reacts.

Unspoken dialogue can be tricky. You don't want the NPC to parrot the unspoken line of dialogue so that the player knows what is said. That's unnatural, especially if the NPC does it more than once or twice. *Lassie* comes to mind, where Timmy asks things like, "What's that, girl? You say 'Mr. Robbins lost his hoe down the well'?" Lassie confirms, "RUFF!" But you also don't want the NPC's response to the unspoken line to be so vague that that player can't figure it out. There needs to be the right amount of context in the NPC's response for the player to figure out the line of dialogue:

> **GRAVY** (Happy): I'm with the WWW. Sher you've heard of us.
>
> **PC**: [Unspoken dialogue.]
>
> **GRAVY** (Flustered): No, not like "World Wide Web."

Use lines of unspoken dialogue sparingly. It can be frustrating not being able to read or hear the player character. And even with fixed characters, they can say something the player disagrees with. However, if the game has a customizable character (i.e., a character where the player determines any of its attributes), or the player has dialogue choices, you want to be careful not to "put words" into the player's mouth. It can be immersion breaking if those words aren't what players would choose for their characters. After all, the PC is the player's in-game representation.

Why, then, would we consider unspoken lines of dialogue for fixed characters? Many games *do* have silent player characters. When the player character is unseen and the player has to imagine the PC being engaged in the world, unspoken dialogue helps to ground the PC in that world. It makes the PC more than just a sounding board for NPCs because the PC engages with them, and NPCs react to what they say.

Unspoken dialogue may not be an option for every game, but it can help an unseen PC feel more "real."

---

office tempts: text boxes and color

I'm currently working on my own game project. It takes place in an office and has escape-the-room-like mechanics, where players have to see how items interact with each other to solve puzzles. The office has three NPCs, all of whom have strained relationships with each other.

Instead of simply using dialogue in text boxes, my team and I are designing different types of text boxes modeled after speech ballotons from comics to help convey the characters' tone and mood. The following screenshots are from a prototype. The boss's secretary, Mabel, and the new office manager, Randi, clash as to how the office should be run. Mabel gets prickly when she thinks she's being accused of something.

Don't mess with Randi's cupcakes. Screenshot from *Office Tempts* prototype. Image owned by Toiya Kristen Finley.

There are no character animations, although we're using character portraits and different emotional states. Mabel is energized and angry, so this shows in her words and in the "icy" dialogue text box. The change in shape of the text box suggests that she's more than a little upset about this. The player can feel and see that intense, negative energy.

In another conversation, Mabel attempts to sway the player and get her/his allegiance. She tries to "butter up" the player.

Screenshot from *Office Tempts* prototype. Image owned by Toiya Kristen Finley.

As I said earlier, you can play with text and innovate with it to express all kinds of ideas through dialogue. Here, Mabel shows feigned affection and admiration for the player with the red hearts on either side of "destined for greatness."

conclusion

Even if you're working within strict technological and/or storage capacity limitations, you have a lot of freedom in how you design and write your game's dialogue. If you have the means within your project's scope, you can create a visual language for your game through the dialogue-text-box design, font choice, font color, etc. This communicates characterization, mood, and the sound of the character's voice. In addition, it gives players a visual language they don't often see in games.

functional dialogue checklist

Determine the best way to deliver dialogue. You and your team should consider the maximum number of characters for each line, the design of the text boxes, and the formatting of the text. Also, what is the best way to position text boxes and character portraits on the screen if you're using cutscenes?

Give every line of dialogue a purpose. Dialogue needs a clear function, whether it's instructional/informational or for character development.

Use dialogue to suggest time and space. If the player character has no in-game representation, think of ways dialogue can tell players where they're situated in the world.

revising functional dialogue

Look at the Following as You Write and Revise Functional Dialogue:

- What is the function of this line of dialogue?
  - Is that clear, first and foremost?

- Is the function stated succinctly?
  - Can you edit out words, restate phrases, or use better word choice?
- Does the character's personality come through?
  - Could any character say this the way the dialogue is written?
  - Rewrite the dialogue if any character could say it.
- Is there better word choice *for this particular character*?
  - Would this character use slang?
  - Would this character use elevated language?
  - What does this character's accent sound like?

i seek the grail
(in five minutes or less)
designing and writing quests
for mobile games

Jessica Sliwinski

contents

introduction

What is your quest? Much like Sir Robin facing the Bridgekeeper, mobile game writers are left with little time to answer. While PC and console games assume the player is sitting in his own home with at least a few hours to sacrifice, mobile games are typically played under an entirely different set of circumstances. The player may be killing time waiting for class to start. She may be taking a break from a hectic workday. He may be trying to distract a small child before the plane boards. For a mobile game, every play session lives and dies on borrowed time—and the player must always feel it is worth the risk.

Though the iPhone may be a far cry from the monochromatic screen of the first Game Boy, when it comes to mobile games, the iPhone is a direct descendant. Early mobile devices served single, specific functions: a Game Boy was for playing games, and a phone was for making calls. Hardware specs that would be laughable by today's standards forced game developers to go small or go home. Quests were short, content was light, and every byte was analyzed for how essential it was to the player's experience. In contrast, today's mobile devices serve multiple functions and are capable of nearly everything a PC or console is. Accordingly, the App Store has seen an influx in both ported PC/console games and new mobile games that make the most of better hardware and longer play sessions.

But even if there are many people settling in for a night of iPad Pro gaming, mobile game writers must take care to remember the primary function of a mobile device: to allow the user to be mobile. Players must be able to pause the game at any time to pay the cashier, answer a call, enter the doctor's office, or just get back to work. If their time is limited (and thus at a premium), players must feel they have spent it wisely and fruitfully. A long dungeon crawl with a major boss at the end that allows no opportunity for the player to pause or save his progress along the way simply won't work.

general theory and best practices: designing mobile game quests

So, what does work? What are the basic elements of a good mobile game quest? We will answer this question in two parts: we will examine basic principles for *designing* quests, and then examine basic principles for *writing* quests (see "I'm a Writer, Not a Designer!" sidebar).

I'm a Writer, Not a Designer!

As a game writer or prospective game writer, you may be wondering why you would need to know anything about quest design—doesn't the designer do that?

When it comes to mobile games, the answer is quite often no. Mobile game studios typically have a far smaller headcount compared to AAA game studios, and often cannot afford to differentiate between a designer and a writer. You may be asked to design quest or mission systems from scratch if hired as a narrative designer or writer on a mobile game, and if you have no prior experience with quest system design, the information provided in this chapter will help you get started.

Even if quest design does not end up being your responsibility, better game writing comes from better understanding of the game itself. Learning more about what goes into designing a quest will help you write more immersive and appropriate text to go with it.

First, we must define what we mean when we use the term *quest*. In his book *Quests: Design, Theory, and History in Games and Narrative*, Jeff Howard provides what may be the best philosophical definition:

> A *quest* is a journey across a symbolic, fantastic landscape in which a protagonist collects objects and talks to characters in order to overcome challenges and achieve a meaningful goal.*

Practically, we can translate this into industry parlance as

> A quest is an objective given to the player that moves him or her through the game space via interactions with objects and/ or NPCs and/or systems in the game. Success achieving said objective results in player progression toward completing and/ or mastering the game.

---

* Jeff Howard, *Quests: Design, Theory, and History in Games and Narrative* (Boca Raton, FL: CRC Press, 2008), xi.

A quest for any genre of game on any platform will meet this definition and include these elements. Thus, when designing a quest, we must answer the following questions:

- *Where does the quest take place?* Note that this does not always mean a fictional location within the game. To say a quest takes place in the Bog of Eternal Stench is only the most cursory, player-facing answer to this question. What level is the player by this point? What skills has he learned (or has yet to learn)? Is this quest branch dependent on a prerequisite earned earlier in the game? Perhaps the quest does not take place in any fictional location, but rather within a menu or system that is part of the game. To turn the question back on the designer: what parts of the game do I want to make the player engage with via this quest?

- *What does the quest ask the player to do?* In other words, what is the player's objective? Is she seeking a rare and powerful object? Trying to unlock a sealed door? Rescuing a duke in distress? Again, these objectives are not solely driven by narrative. The player may be trying to unlock a game feature, hit a certain level, or accomplish a statistically based achievement.

- *How will the player complete this quest?* What actions will the player need to perform in order to complete this quest? This question should be considered in light of the entire timeline of a quest: How will the player obtain this quest? How will he monitor his progress while attempting to complete it? And, when complete, how will he notify the game in exchange for the promised rewards? Most often, we think of engaging in combat or speaking to an NPC, or interacting with an in-game object (example, turn the windmill). But these actions involve many sub-actions. When a player is asked to engage in combat, he does not only attack an enemy but also engages with the inventory system to equip himself with the best gear (and perhaps the game shop if his gear is not good enough). He reviews his character record to ensure he is as statistically powerful as possible. He reads the lorebook to ensure he knows everything about the challenge he is about to face. When designing quests, we must consider not only what that means narratively, but also in terms of actual gameplay, on the other side of the fourth wall.

- *What obstacles will the player face in completing this quest?* Obstacles are perhaps the most important part of the equation. Just as conflict is the primary fuel source for a good story, so too is it the primary fuel source for good gameplay. If the player wants something, and the path to obtaining that something is as simple as opening a menu or reading a lorebook entry, the game is over. Again, obstacles are not necessarily just aggressive beasts or impassable terrain. Obstacles can include depletion of needed resources, beating an in-game clock, or the unpredictable actions of other players.

When it comes to designing quests for *mobile* games, however, there are more specific and useful ways to approach these questions that will help us understand how designing quests for mobile games can differ from other platforms:

Where does the quest take place? → *What is the core loop of the game?*

The *core loop* is the chain of actions the player will repeat most often as part of playing the game, and should represent its most rewarding and addictive play. The most commonly cited example of a core loop is in Namco's classic arcade game *Pac-Man*, which can be defined as

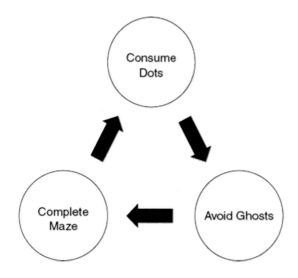

In BioWare's *Mass Effect*, the core loop might be defined as

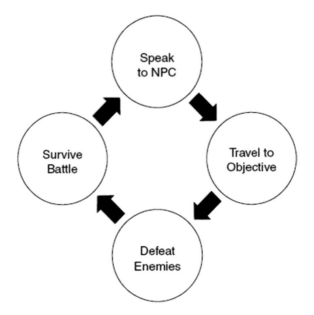

A game can also have several secondary loops in addition to the core loop. In *Mass Effect*, these might include

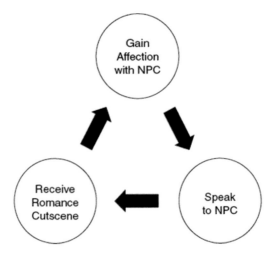

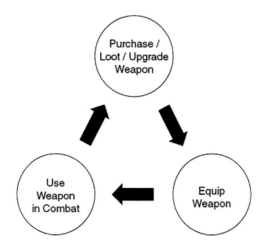

This is par for the course in sprawling, epic console games. But mobile games, by nature simpler and more lightweight than games on other platforms, often consist entirely of a single core loop. Take the core loop of King's *Candy Crush Saga*, for example, which can be defined as

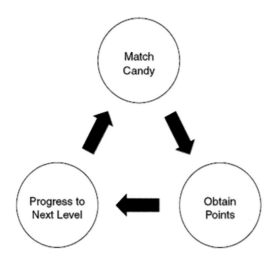

Or Blizzard's *Hearthstone*, which might be defined as

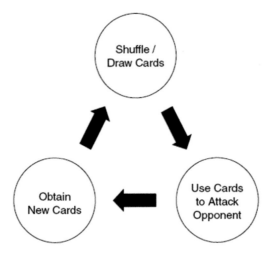

Thus, in a mobile game, the core loop becomes more important than ever when designing quests, particularly in determining where they take place in the game space. A *Pac-Man* quest that does not require the player to traverse a maze, a *Candy Crush Saga* quest that does not ask the player to match candy, or a *Hearthstone* quest that does not involve cards are not encouraging the player to engage in the game's core loop.

What does the quest ask the player to do? → *Is the reward worth the effort for the player?*

As discussed, the mobile game player's time is often stolen or at a premium. The player must feel as though that time was well spent at the end of a play session. Thus, quest objectives must involve meaningful progression toward the player's goals. Moving from the first floor of the evil villain's skyscraper to the second will seem like an exercise in futility to a player who only has 10 minutes a day to devote to the game. Defeating the evil villain's second-in-command, however, gives the player both a feeling of satisfaction and accomplishment, as well as the motivation to keep playing.

Consider what the player gets out of completing a quest in a practical sense as well: in Disruptor Beam's *Star Trek*

Timelines, merits are routinely awarded to the player for completing most any task in the game. A quest in which the main objective or ultimate reward is to obtain merits, then, will not seem like a worthy use of the player's time. Crew members, however, such as Captain Jean-Luc Picard or Lieutenant Commander Worf, can only be purchased with Dilithium—the game's premium currency. A quest that promises the player a new crew member as his reward is a much more enticing proposition.

How will the player complete this quest? → *What role will the game economy play?*

The word "economy" may first conjure images of dollars and cents, storefronts, and goods for sale. But while these are certainly elements of a game's economy, it also includes all those nontraditional "currencies" used as checks and balances to control the player's pace. Energy, resources, enemy/player stats, and timers are all part of a game's economy too. When designing quests for a mobile game, we must consider: What will the player need to acquire or spend in order to complete this quest? Can it be acquired or spent in the same number of sessions it will take the player to complete the quest? Or have I inadvertently doubled the amount of effort I intended to require?

In Disruptor Beam's *Game of Thrones Ascent*, the player has a stable of Sworn Swords she can use to complete quests. Once Sworn Swords are sent on a quest, they are unavailable for a period of time. The player is given one Sworn Sword as a reward for completing the game's prologue, but more can only be obtained by spending in-game currency. If the player receives two quests requiring her to commit Sworn Swords early in the game, she can only complete one with the single Sworn Sword at her disposal. If she wants to complete the other, she must either wait for her single Sworn Sword to successfully complete the first quest, or procure a second Sworn Sword. Mobile game quest designers must consider these economical hierarchies if we are to create a satisfying experience for the player.

What obstacles will the player face in completing this quest? →
How much time does the player have in a typical play session?

As we have established, the pace at which a player moves through a mobile game differs greatly from the pace at which he moves through a console or PC game. Mobile games are played multiple times a day for short periods of time, while console/PC games are played less times a day but for much longer durations. Additionally, while many console/PC games also offer multiplayer or other social systems, mobile games as a genre are far more likely to feature these types of systems, making the player's time investment potentially even more critical: juggling multiple schedules to get a player and his friends online at the same time is difficult! We have already stressed the importance of not wasting the player's borrowed time and ensuring these play sessions feel worth the sacrifice. But we can only accomplish these goals if the player can complete a quest. The most frustrating experience we could create is one in which 10 stolen minutes are spent in defeat after defeat after defeat, with nothing to show for it but depleted resources and lost time.

In the late Zynga game *The Ville*, players inhabit a *Sims*-like world in which all quest objectives revolve around expanding and furnishing their lot. After an initial narrative intro, the game gives the player a straightforward visual summary of quest objectives, thus ensuring he fully understands what is being asked of him and what will be required to accomplish it. A brief narrative summary ensures that the player will always be aware of the context for completing these objectives. Finally, the game breaks down the objectives into numbered actions or items that can be completed or obtained at least once within a single play session, thus ensuring that the player's valuable time will not be wasted.

In *Game of Thrones Ascent*, boss quests are generously timed, three-act quests that allow the player to take five actions at regular intervals until the quest's timer elapses. If the player is racing against the clock, he may either immediately purchase more actions, thus moving the quest to successful completion faster, or request aid from friends, who can then log into the game at their leisure, open their friend's quest, and take actions of their own to help their friend complete it more quickly, at no cost to themselves or their friend, save the time investment. This system not only encourages social behaviors but also respects the time of all players involved.

---

general theory and best practices: writing mobile game quests

Now that we understand how to design good mobile game quests, we can delve more deeply into how to *write* good mobile game quests. All of the driving questions identified above for the designer are just as critical for the writer; the answers simply use a different medium. Let's revisit these questions from the writer's point of view.

What is the core loop of the game?

Just as quest gameplay must incorporate and reinforce the core loop of the game, so too must quest text. This does not mean the writer must produce forced, "gamey" dialogue that strings objectives together or breaks the fourth wall to refer the player to certain buttons or objects. Rather, it means that the writer must always take care to answer narrative questions with a piece of the core loop.

For example, if we look again at *Star Trek Timelines*, the core loop could be summed up thusly:

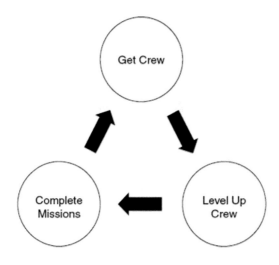

Despite its more "mature" usage of the *Star Trek* IP, *Star Trek Timelines* is, at its core, a creature collection game. In this case, the "creatures" are actually beloved *Star Trek* characters, such as Captain Kirk and Doctor McCoy. While there are many canonically appropriate reasons for a Starfleet captain to spend the majority of his time recruiting and training his crew, most creature collection games thrive on the concept that the creatures are rare and difficult to find, whether by intentional avoidance of the player or simply because they're lost and confused. The narrative of *Star Trek Timelines* reinforces this concept by stating that a series of temporal anomalies have transported beloved *Star Trek* characters across space and time. Only the player has the wherewithal to locate these characters and return them to active duty.

Is the reward worth the effort for the player?

The narrative of a mobile game should reinforce not only the core loop but also the hierarchy of rewards in the game. If weapons are the most important and valuable items in the game, the narrative should not revolve around the building of a base; it should revolve around the acquisition and retention of weapons as a proactive means of defending that base.

In mobile games, valuable items or currency are often not doled out with the same frequency as they are in a PC or console game. Often, they are not doled out at all, but sold as microtransactions. This can feel unfair to some players, who feel as though many mobile games are constantly asking them to open their wallets, or are, in essence, "pay to win." But narrative can be a powerful balm for these feelings; solving a mystery, resolving a cliffhanger, introducing a popular character from an established IP, and revealing the fallout of a player decision are all rewards worthy of a player's effort, and often cheap to implement since they typically have little to no impact on a mobile game's core loop or economy. The writer should thus be mindful of pacing the story to reward the player's time investment, saving events such as those listed above for the end of a play session or the completion of a particularly difficult quest. (For more on narrative design in free-to-play games, please see Chapter 12, "Buy Gems to Woo Your Lover: Free-to-Play Narratives.")

Using *Game of Thrones Ascent* as an example again, arguably the most narratively meaningful moments in the game are when the player interacts with major characters from HBO's hit series, such as Ned Stark or Tyrion Lannister. During the prologue volume, which also serves as the tutorial to the game, interactions with these characters are wisely reserved for the end of the volume, as opposed to the beginning. After undergoing the sometimes onerous tutorial experience common to most games, the *Game of Thrones Ascent* player is rewarded for his hard work with personal one-on-one time with a major character tied to his or her favorite house, personally selected by the player at an earlier point in the prologue.

What role will the game economy play?

Remember that the game economy encompasses more than dollars and cents. It also encompasses energy, time, ingredients, or other nonmonetary resources. All quests demand a portion of these resources, and it is important for the writer to be aware of these demands and write fiction to match. A quest that demands a minor amount of resources but is fictionalized as the final battle against the main antagonist is dissonant at best and wasteful at worst. Conversely, a quest that demands a huge amount of resources but is fictionalized as a minor fetch quest to retrieve an item for a random NPC is disrespectful to the player and his time investment into the game. Whenever possible, the writer must ensure that the mobile game quest narrative justifies the quest requirements.

Looking once more at *Star Trek Timelines*, crew, such as Commander Spock or Captain Janeway, are the most valuable items in the game. Each character is classified on a star system, with five-star characters being the most powerful in the game. Thus, five-star characters are rarely rewarded for free—and when they are, it requires a significant effort on the part of the player. To receive the two-star Security Chief Worf, the player need only complete "Episode 1," which is available immediately after completion of the game's tutorial and is considered easy difficulty.

To receive the four-star Commander Tomalak character—four stars being the second most powerful type of character in the game—the player must complete "Episodes 1–7," an amount of effort equivalent to the value of the associated reward.

How much time does the player have in a typical play session?

Though it arguably takes far less time to read quest dialogue than it takes to complete the quest, the writer must still respect the mobile game player's valuable and limited time. Text must not be overly long, take multiple taps to get through, or require intense analysis to be understood. Pacing must be brisk and even. The player must be reminded of key objectives, plot points, and characters in the event that his last play session was some time ago. The mobile game writer should consider the mobile game player on a need-to-know basis: what is the minimum amount of information the player needs to complete this quest in a single play session?

Blizzard's *Hearthstone* is an excellent example of narrative presented on a need-to-know basis. Though *Hearthstone* is part of the larger *World of Warcraft* universe, and the characters in *Hearthstone* may have extensive histories, the player doesn't need to know any of that to engage one character against another in a card battle. Some banter to establish character personalities and occasional explanation of a new mechanic are all that are necessary.

Now that we have reviewed best practices for both mobile game quest design and writing, we can take a closer look at three titles that have put these best practices into action, with great success.

case studies: introduction

Each case study in this chapter examines a game that is currently or has previously been in the "Top Grossing Apps" chart in the iOS

App Store. This is not to say that only games that make a great deal of money can teach us anything, but after making one great game, a company also needs to make a profit in order to make the next one. The developers of these games, who range from small independent companies to large corporations, are clearly doing something right.

All of the games featured in this chapter also utilize the *freemium* pricing strategy. A *freemium* game is one in which the player may download, install, and play the game for free, but may also choose to unlock premium features, additional functionality, and/or high-quality virtual goods via microtransaction. Again, this is not to say that only freemium games have well-written quests, but an acknowledgement of the fact that freemium is the dominant (and arguably, the most successful) model in the history of mobile game development thus far.

Case Study #1: *Farmville 2: Country Escape* (2014)

We begin with Zynga, one of the great-grandfathers of the mobile game industry. Mobile games are the direct descendants of web games, which, like handheld games, catered to players looking for a quick break from any location with access to a web browser. Accordingly, Zynga designed their web games for players who were short on time and hungry for bite-sized entertainment and, in doing so, established many of the rules and best practices for mobile game quest design still being followed today.

Our first case study, *FarmVille 2: Country Escape*, is a reimagining of Zynga's blockbuster web game, *FarmVille.* Like its predecessor, *FarmVille 2: Country Escape* is a farming simulation aimed at casual iOS, Android, and Windows Phone gamers. The player's narrative introduction to the game is short and sweet: he has inherited a farm from his grandparents, and their old farmhand friend Marie has promised to help the player learn all he needs to see it flourish. Within the first few seconds of gameplay, *FarmVille 2* is already respecting the player's time by telling him no more than he needs to know to get started. The player has a farm, it came from his grandparents, and Marie is there to tell him how to take care of it.

Marie, the player's main quest giver, shows him around the farm. Screenshot from *Farmville 2: Country Escape*. Developed/published by Zynga and is protected by United States and international copyright law. © Zynga

From there, the player's very first actions in the game are appropriately part of its core loop. The core loop of *FarmVille 2: Country Escape* could be represented as follows:

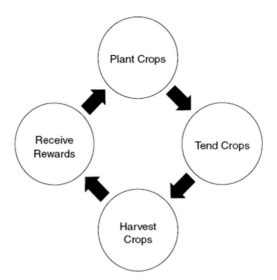

The player begins engagement in this loop on "Tend Crops," as the farm he inherits already has two wheat plots and an apple tree, just waiting for the player's green thumb. Marie instructs the player on how to water these crops to promote their growth, how to use Keys (*FarmVille 2*'s premium currency) to speed up said growth, and, finally, how to harvest the crops and sell them for Coins (*FarmVille 2*'s nonpremium currency) and experience points (XP). Again, in only a few more steps, *FarmVille 2* incorporates both the game's core loop and a secondary loop for premium currency into the narrative.

Marie simultaneously instructs the player on how to engage with the core loop and how to use premium currency. Screenshot from *Farmville 2: Country Escape*. Developed/published by Zynga and is protected by United States and international copyright law. © Zynga

Shortly afterward, the player unlocks the Quest Book, the organizational feature through which he will receive quests and progress through the game. Each quest is broken down into a series of objectives that contribute toward an overall narrative goal. Each objective is either broken down further into tasks that can be accomplished or started in a single play session, or naturally completed as a result of finishing earlier objectives. If the player holds a finger down on the objective, he will receive a helpful tooltip giving him further instruction on how to complete it. Rewards for completing the quest are clearly displayed on the same screen as both narrative and objectives.

A quest in *Farmville 2: Country Escape.* Screenshot from *Farmville 2: Country Escape.* Developed/published by Zynga and is protected by United States and international copyright law. © Zynga

Once again, *FarmVille 2* shows respect for the player's time. The player is given all the information he needs to set about completing the objectives for a quest, thus ensuring he doesn't waste valuable seconds trying to puzzle it out. The player's objectives are broken down into bite-sized chunks, and no matter where the player chooses to start, he will always make progress toward the overall goal. The player's reward is equal to the amount of effort required, a small amount of XP in exchange for completing tasks and objectives that take less than 1–5 minutes to complete individually. Most importantly, the player is engaging with the core loop over and over again as a result of working toward completing the quest. If these elements seem familiar and even obvious today, it is all thanks to Zynga's early efforts, which allowed them to perfect the design for their own eventual foray into the mobile space.

But Zynga has a few new tricks, too. The quest givers of *FarmVille 2* are always sure to congratulate the player on his progress and/or accomplishments. In a multipart quest or quest chain, the quest givers also often hint at the next exciting part of the story to come and potential rewards to be earned.

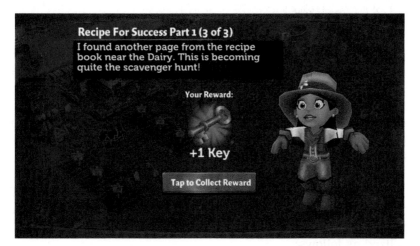

Story rewards, currency rewards, and the promise of more to come in *Farmville 2: Country Escape*. Screenshot from *Farmville 2: Country Escape*. Developed/published by Zynga and is protected by United States and international copyright law. © Zynga

In an industry sometimes dominated by dark heroism and the desire to challenge the player more than reward him, *FarmVille 2: Country Escape*'s optimism and continual promise of sunnier days for the player serve both as positive motivation and true escapism.

Case Study #2: *The Simpsons: Tapped Out* (2012)

Licensed products,* by nature of their more complicated approvals processes and desired marketing synchronization with similar products, often run the risk of being inauthentic and/or poorly designed. *The Simpsons: Tapped Out* (EA) is neither, an exceptional licensed product based on Fox's hit animated show, which not only evokes its source material but also is addictively well-designed. The premise of *The Simpsons: Tapped Out* connects itself to the player's experience in a very literal way: Homer Simpson himself is playing a mobile game when he neglects his duties at the Springfield Nuclear Power Plant, inadvertently destroying the entire town of Springfield, which the player is then tasked with reconstructing as they see fit. This narrative is communicated to the player via an

---

* For more on working with licensed IP, see "The Continued Adventures: Writing for Licensed Games" (Chapter 10).

opening cinematic written, voiced, and animated in the same style as *The Simpsons* television show itself. Like *FarmVille 2: Country Escape, The Simpsons: Tapped Out* shows respect for the mobile player's limited time by keeping the game's introduction short and sweet, and both the player's presumed familiarity with the character of Homer Simpson as well as Homer's initial actions circumvent the need to explain why the player is compelled to assist him. Homer Simpson is clearly not intellectually capable of rebuilding the town of Springfield on his own; only you can ensure the town and all its beloved inhabitants are restored.

The Simpsons: Tapped Out is primarily a city-building game, with a secondary emphasis on creature (or in this case, *The Simpsons* character) collection. The core loop of *The Simpsons: Tapped Out* might be visualized as follows:

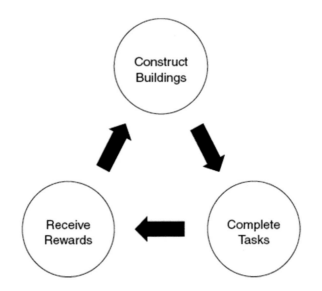

The core loop is integrated directly into the game's premise. Thanks to Homer's negligence at the nuclear power plant, the town of Springfield has been reduced to an empty field. It will only be restored if the player reconstructs it, building by building. Once constructed, each building begins to produce resources and rewards, which the player can then use to fund the construction of more buildings. The player is not simply dumped into a sandbox where all buildings are available to him at once, however. Buildings are tied to characters who have also gone missing in the wake of the destruction. The player's very first construction tasks are narratively motivated by these characters; Homer stands alone in a crater of his making, his wife Marge and children Bart, Lisa, and Maggie nowhere to be found. He states his desire to be reunited with them, not least of all because some of them will know better how to handle this crisis. By reconstructing the Simpson family's home, the player instantly grants Homer's wish: daughter Lisa is located and unlocked for the player's use as part of construction. However, *The Simpsons: Tapped Out* is mindful of these characters' value to the player (both as gameplay objects and as beloved characters) and times their unlocks accordingly. Apu, the owner of the Kwik-E-Mart and a relatively minor character, is unlocked as part of the game tutorial, while Bart Simpson—arguably the most popular member of the Simpson family—is not unlocked until the player reaches level 12. Unlocking Bart as part of the game tutorial would not be making the most of this character's perceived value, while unlocking Apu at level 12 would feel like a paltry reward for the player's efforts. Characters are also grouped together into like collections; for instance, the entire Simpson family is grouped into a single collection, giving the player a sense of progression even if he has only unlocked one or two members of the Simpson family, and a greater sense of satisfaction when he is finally able to reunite Homer, Marge, Bart, Lisa, Maggie, and Grandpa Simpson later in the game.

From Apu's Kwik-E-Mart shifts to Bart's skateboarding, each character has a suite of timed actions that can be performed at the player's direction. Some take only a few moments, while others can take hours or even days. Accordingly, actions of a longer duration result in greater rewards, showing consideration for the time and effort the player has expended. These actions are character specific, often direct callbacks to scenes or episodes of the show, and together they grant the player a powerful feeling of agency. The player may choose to assign actions according to best narrative flow, desired rewards pursuant to an overall goal, or current play session length. Timers allow the player to put the game down and pick it back up several times over the course of the day, in keeping with most mobile game players' typical play schedules. These actions also breathe life into every player's reconstructed Springfield, regardless of individual progress. Marge Simpson can be seen protesting on the streets, while her son Bart skateboards outside school. Homer lounges in an inner tube in his backyard, while Apu attempts to feed his octuplets.

While the player can assign characters to perform actions at will, they are also organized into ongoing quest chains, which guide the player from Springfield's initial destruction through his rebuilding efforts. While many quest objectives involve directing characters to take specific actions, many also ask the player to construct specific buildings, thus directly reinforcing both the game's core and secondary loops. The player's initial efforts to rebuild Springfield are directed by the whims and desires of the Simpson family, but as more and more Springfieldians are recovered, the player learns that they all have their own agendas and opinions—like Krusty the Clown, who would very much appreciate it if the player would reconstruct his eponymous Krusty Burger ASAP. But what if the player doesn't care for Krusty as a character or doesn't currently desire the resources and rewards reconstructing the Krusty Burger would bring? He can either simply ignore the quest chain until a later date and direct the characters' actions outside its directives, or choose to pursue a concurrently available quest chain. There is no danger of the player losing track of an available quest or forgetting it exists: characters will roam the streets holding large exclamation points over their heads in an effort to get the player's attention.

The flexibility of *The Simpsons: Tapped Out*'s quest and character action systems is a hallmark of the well-designed mobile game: by providing multiple quest chains with multiple objectives, each attached to timed actions of varying length and effort, as well as the ability to ignore the quest system entirely, players may tailor their play sessions by whatever criteria maximize their enjoyment of the game.

Case Study #3: *Pearl's Peril* (2013)

We have thus far examined best practices for mobile game quest design and writing in terms of simulators, city builders, and creature collection game genres. Wooga's *Pearl's Peril* affords us a look at these practices in terms of the wildly popular hidden object genre, in which players are presented with intricately illustrated scenes and asked to locate specific objects within them. Before delving into the game's narrative premise, however, we should examine its core loop, which informs that premise even more organically than either of our previous case studies. The core loop of *Pearl's Peril* could be summed up thusly:

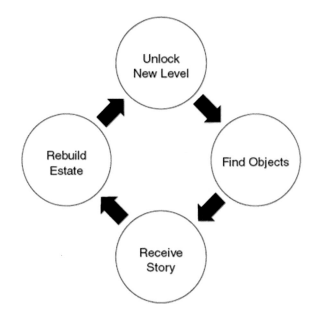

Like our other case study games, *Pearl's Peril* is something of a hybrid, primarily a hidden-object game with a secondary city-building loop. There is nothing mysterious about city building. Its very nature suggests the unavoidable noise and bother of a construction site. But the core loop of *Pearl's Peril* revolves around finding hidden objects, which is mysterious indeed. Who hid these possessions? Why is no one besides the player able to locate them? Why is it important that they be found? There could be many fictional motivations to rebuilding an estate: additional income, community revitalization, a promise made to a loved one. The makers of *Pearl's Peril* instead choose a very specific narrative premise that reinforces every aspect of its core loop: Pearl's father, owner of a sprawling estate, has died under mysterious circumstances (Unlock New Level), leaving the estate to degrade over time (Rebuild Estate). Pearl, as his next of kin, is the natural choice to go through his effects (Find Objects), and personally invested in learning the circumstances of his death (Receive Story). Thus, the question of the player's motivation—i.e., "Why should I search for these objects and/ or rebuild this estate?"—is answered in a way that reinforces the core loop: "Rebuilding the estate will help Pearl locate and organize her father's possessions, which will in turn reveal clues that could solve the mystery of his death."

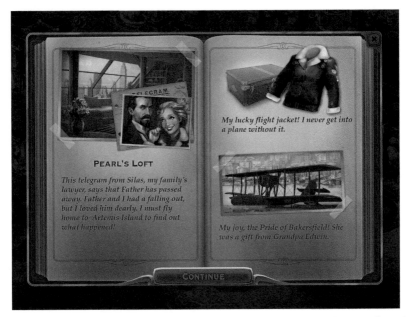

Pearl writes of her father's death and the significance of objects. Screenshot from *Pearl's Peril* developed and published by Wooga. © Wooga

In a hidden object game, where the player's primary satisfaction is derived from locating objects, the most valuable reward is a new scene in which to search for said objects. In *Pearl's Peril*, these scenes are organized into chapters, and the process by which the player progresses through them may be considered the game's quest system. A chapter cannot be completed until all hidden objects have been located in each scene within. Scenes may be unlocked by acquiring a specified quantity of a specified resource. Resources are obtained from various buildings on the reconstructed estate. Constructing a new building on the estate has its own set of requirements, which may be met in turn by successfully locating objects in various scenes. Thus, unlocking a new scene—let alone an entirely new chapter—constitutes a fair amount of work on the player's part. *Pearl's Peril* wisely utilizes both the overarching narrative and the perceived value of new scenes as motivators for the player. If the player continues to unlock new scenes, he will not only receive the physical reward of a scene in which to search for new objects, but also will continue to unravel the mystery of Pearl's father's death. Each new narrative twist in Pearl's investigation is revealed only *after* the player has successfully completed a chapter, thus rewarding the player's significant time investment both in terms of story and gameplay.

The estate, awaiting restoration to its former glory. Screenshot from *Pearl's Peril* developed and published by Wooga. © Wooga

While like most city-building systems, estate construction in *Pearl's Peril* takes varying amounts of time, this is not the primary pacing mechanism of the game. Opening a scene to search for hidden objects also consumes energy. The player can generate a fixed amount of energy over time, but once this is consumed, the player must wait for it to regenerate before she can search a scene again. The nature of hidden object gameplay in tandem with the energy system gradually assumes *Pearl's Peril* players will be able to accommodate longer play sessions: the player must be reasonably confident she can locate all the hidden objects in a scene within the current play session, or she will have wasted her energy on a failed search.

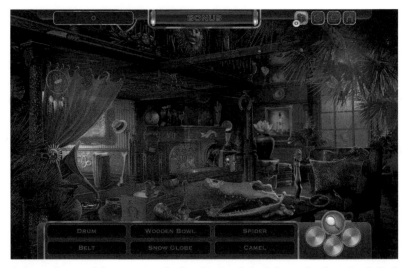

A cluttered room of clues waiting to be found in *Pearl's Peril*. Screenshot from *Pearl's Peril* developed and published by Wooga. © Wooga

Thankfully, *Pearl's Peril* does not require the player to locate all objects in a scene within a specific time frame. Though a timer is present, it is purely for personal benchmarking and record setting. Still, the narrative designers and artists who create the scenes must be mindful both of the story they are trying to tell, as well as the overall difficulty in finding the scene's hidden objects. Too difficult, and the player risks wasting time. Too easy, and the player will be left unsatisfied. The success of *Pearl's Peril* proves that Wooga has achieved the elusive balance between pacing a game for the mobile player while still providing a satisfying experience.

conclusion

All games differ by virtue of their platform. A game of freeze tag cannot be played as effectively inside as it can be played outside. A game of rock–paper–scissors cannot be played in the same time frame as a game of Monopoly. Videogames are no exception. The mobile game player desires the freedom to play anywhere, anytime, without restriction or penalty. The mobile game designer seeks to accommodate them with gameplay that encourages multiple, shorter play sessions. The mobile quest designer and writer can further support these efforts by reinforcing the game's core loop (particularly in the game's narrative premise), ensuring rewards (whether story or gameplay based) are in sync with the player's level of effort, making the game's most valuable items central to the story, and always respecting the player's time via flexible quest systems and objectives. Whether planting carrots, rebuilding a town, or searching for clues, any mobile game that features good quest design and writing will become an anticipated part of a player's day. As far as when or where... well, that's up to the player.

as you prepare to write, ask yourself the following:

For Any Game:

Where does the quest take place? Note that this does not only mean a fictional location within the game. Player progression, UX flow, and what systems the player will engage with in order to complete this quest are things to consider when answering this question.

What does the quest ask the player to do? Again, this does not only refer to the player's narrative objective. Completing the quest may accomplish other nonnarrative goals, such as unlocking a new system, item, or achievement.

How will the player complete this quest? Most often, we think of engaging in combat, or speaking to an NPC, or interacting with an in-game object. But these actions involve many subactions. This question should be considered in light of the entire timeline of a quest, from acquisition to completion.

What obstacles will the player face in completing this quest? Just as conflict is the primary fuel source for a good story, so too is it the primary fuel source for good gameplay. Remember that obstacles do not just mean difficult terrain or enemies; they also can include depletion of needed resources, beating an in-game clock, or the unpredictable actions of other players.

For Mobile Games:

What is the core loop of the game? The core loop is the chain of actions the player will repeat most often as part of playing the game and should represent its most rewarding and addictive play. Mobile games often consist entirely of a single core loop.

Is the reward worth the effort for the player? The mobile game player's time is often stolen or at a premium. The player must feel as though that time was well spent at the end of a play session. Thus, quest objectives must involve meaningful progression toward the player's goals.

What role will the game economy play? The economy does not only include traditional currencies and microtransactional storefronts, but also nontraditional "currencies" used as checks and balances to control the player's pace, such as energy, resources, enemy/player stats, and timers.

How much time does the player have in a typical play session? Mobile games are played multiple times a day for short periods of time, potentially while juggling schedules with friends to participate in multiplayer or social game systems. Satisfaction comes when the player is always able to complete a goal (say, a quest) in one of these play sessions.

as you revise, ask yourself the following:

- Is the player's motivation something that reinforces the core loop of the game?
  - The core loop should be the most enjoyable and often repeated series of actions in the game, and any narrative that fails to constantly reintroduce the player to that loop does a disservice to the game as a whole.
- Does the narrative support the game's definition of valuable and nonvaluable items, or does it contradict it?
  - Whenever natural and possible, game narrative should extol the virtues of the game's most valuable items. Narrative dissonance with the game economy can undermine the work of systems designers and create misperceptions about that economy.
- Do the narrative stakes match the amount of effort the player will need to expend to complete the quest?

- In the same vein as the question above, the grandeur of the narrative should not significantly exceed or fall short of the time the player will need to invest in order to complete a quest. Spending hours to deliver a warm cup of coffee to a waiting superior doesn't feel satisfying. Spending hours to save that superior's life does!

- Are climaxes, reveals, and other "valuable" narrative moments timed to coincide with an expenditure of significant effort from the player?

  - Narrative is as much a reward as any powerful item or ability, and should not be easily obtained if highly valuable. The best narrative rewards should be timed to create a well-paced, satisfying player experience.

- Are the player's objectives and how to complete them clearly communicated?

  - The player's time and patience are at a premium in mobile gaming. Respect that time by not making the player waste it puzzling out what the game wants her to do.

- Does each string contain only essential information, nothing more?

  - Are all strings as short as possible while remaining informative and interesting? This is not to say that every string in a mobile game should be dry exposition or lack character. Rather, that the mobile game writer should again respect the player's time by not making him sift through many ultimately meaningless asides in order to get to the meat of a sentence. Omit needless words!

references and recommended reading

Candy Crush Saga. Stockholm: King, 2012. Videogame.

Cook, Adrian. (2017). "Designing Core Loops" (blog). *Adrian Crook & Associates.* Last modified July 24, 2012. http://adriancrook.com/designing-core-loops/

Despain, Wendy. *Writing for Video Game Genres: From FPS to RPG.* 1st ed. Wellesley, MA: A.K. Peters, 2008.

Despain, Wendy, ed. *Professional Techniques for Video Game Writing.* 1st ed. Wellesley, MA: A.K. Peters, 2009.

FarmVille 2: Country Escape. San Francisco: Zynga, 2014. Videogame.

Fields, Tim. *Mobile & Social Game Design: Monetization Methods and Mechanics.* 1st ed. Boca Raton, FL: CRC Press, 2014.

Gamasutra.com. "Video: How to Make Killer Game Loops." Last modified July 20, 2012. http://www.gamasutra.com/view/news /173732/

Game of Thrones Ascent. Framingham, MA: Disruptor Beam, 2013. Videogame.

Hearthstone. Irvine, CA: Blizzard Entertainment, 2014. Videogame.

Heussner, Tobias, Finley, Toiya Kristen, Hepler, Jennifer, and Lemay, Ann. *The Game Narrative Toolbox.* 1st ed. Hoboken, NJ: Taylor & Francis, 2015.

Howard, Jeff. *Quests: Design, Theory, and History in Games and Narratives.* 1st ed. Wellesley, MA: A.K. Peters, 2008.

Katkoff, Michail. "Mid-Core Success Part 1: Core Loops," last modified October 24, 2013. http://www.gamasutra.com/blogs /MichailKatkoff/20131024/203142/MidCore_Success_Part_1 _Core_Loops.php

Mass Effect. Edmonton: BioWare, 2007. Videogame.

Momoda, Jerry. "The Importance of Core Game Loops—Part 2 of 2," *Game Analysis* (blog). Last accessed March 9, 2017. http:// jerrymomoda.com/the-core-loop-the-most-important-part-of-a -video-game-part-2-of-2/

Pac-Man. Tokyo: Namco, 1980. Videogame.

Pearl's Peril. Berlin: Wooga, 2013. Videogame.

Salter, Anastasia. *What Is Your Quest? From Adventure Games to Interactive Books.* 1st ed. Iowa City: University of Iowa Press, 2014.

Schell, Jesse. *The Art of Game Design.* 1st ed. Boca Raton, FL: CRC Press, 2015.

Scolastici, Claudio and Nolte, David. *Mobile Game Design Essentials.* 1st ed. Birmingham, UK: Packt Pub, 2013.

The Simpsons: Tapped Out. (2012). Los Angeles, CA: Electronic Arts, 2012. Videogame.

Star Trek Timelines. Framingham, MA: Disruptor Beam, 2016. Videogame.

The Ville. San Francisco: Zynga, 2012. Videogame.

11

storytelling for different demographics and genres

to each their own
writing for demographics

Megan Fausti

contents

who is your game for?

You've probably heard CEOs of successful game companies say something like, "We're the number one FTP, multiplayer, head-to-head, clicker simulator in our target demographic." Okay, great, but what does that mean for you as a writer? Well, everything and nothing at all.

If you've ever been online, you'll notice a frighteningly boring phenomenon: you've been placed in a demographic. Don't believe me?

Just turn off your ad blocker. Based on your web browsing habits, you're likely to see ads that agencies have deemed "just right" for you, based on a number of qualifications that may or may not be real. For instance, as an unmarried woman in my 20s, if I turn off my ad blocker, I see an inordinate amount of promotions for wedding dresses from out-of-touch advertisers. Thanks, guys.

Okay, cool, but what does this have to do with narrative design? Well, we've already explored a few of the fundamental advantages and flaws of demographics. Let's look at them in more detail.

writing beyond the tropes

The first and most obvious advantage of writing for a specific demographic is that it sets basic parameters. You're not likely to write a complex, interactive memoir of Eva Perón for young children, and it would seem out of place to make a reference to Nicki Minaj's feud with Miley Cyrus in a game aimed at the elderly. Understanding whom you're writing for is a key skill in any art form, and games are no exception.

Another advantage that isn't addressed as much is that it gives you the opportunity to research. While research should be any writer's bread and butter, it's often overlooked as part of the process. This tends to be especially true when the writer is not a member of the demographic for which they're writing. This is a *huge* disconnect that can lead to minor narrative issues or even broader, social concerns. We'll talk more about that shortly. When done correctly, this can be an extremely positive thing for both the writer and the audience. As a writer, you'll grow in your craft and possibly as a person. As for your audience, they'll get the benefit of a writer who took time and care to represent themes they care about. That might not seem like much, but it can make the difference between a "meh" experience and a player's favorite game.

I'm convinced that basically everything in the universe follows Newton's third law. Unfortunately, that means that for every good thing about demographics, there's an equal and opposite bad thing. Depressing, right? There's some good news though: you can avoid all of them, but first we have to name them.

Stereotypes/Tropes

This is both the worst and easiest trap to fall into as a writer. All through our pre-collegiate education, we're taught about the importance of archetypes. We study them with reverence—after all, some of our most iconic and beloved stories are based on them. Our teachers place them on literary pedestals reminding us that all the greats have used them, from Homer to George Lucas. By the time we're ready to start writing professionally, we know these characters implicitly. And it's not just us; our audience members have the same deep understanding of these characters, making it easier for us to neatly interweave them into stories. Let's take the Wise Old Woman/Man for example. We've seen this archetype so often that it's hardly necessary to explain *why* or *how* this person is wise in the first place.

It can therefore be tempting to transfer this idea over to social demographics, especially when we have data that seem to place them in narrowly defined boxes. This line of thinking goes something like, "Our consumer research says young girls like pink and princesses so, to appeal to young girls, we need to make a game about pink-dress-clad princesses." The data tell you "X," and you follow through with "Y." Seems pretty logical—right?

Yikes, no. You've forgotten one of the golden rules of writing: demographics aren't monoliths. Just because you can see a visible trend does not mean you should base all of your creative decisions on it. There's no quicker way to a player's bad side than pandering. This is particularly true with demographics who are often stereotyped—if you rush out a poorly researched female character, you're much more likely to alienate more women than you appease. Let's be clear: this kind of slipshod work isn't just offensive, but it's severely lacking in creativity. Now, this doesn't mean you can't write for characters outside of your experience. You just have to do so with care and empathy. Here are a few basic ground rules:

1. *Treat your demographic like people.* This may seem obvious, but it often gets lost in favor of easily reproduced stereotypes, which, again, are the product of lazy writing.

2. *When making decisions, don't think, "What would minority X like?"* Think about what that character would do. Make detailed character backstories that include all the ways your creations are complicated, interesting, and dynamic.

3. *Places can be stereotyped too.* If you're creating a narrative in modern-day Zimbabwe, don't mash together aspects of other African countries to fulfill stereotypical expectations about what Africa is "supposed" to look like. Take care to research

its economy, leadership, racial/ethnic distribution, and what concerns its citizens have with those factors.

4. *Always do your research!* I can't stress this one enough. If you're not researching before writing, you're not doing your job properly.

5. *Don't steal people's stories and/or profit from their emotional labor.* The first is easy since we all understand the concept of plagiarism, but many people don't understand the second. Profiting from another's emotional labor is essentially abstract plagiarism. It occurs when someone (generally from a majority/dominant group) shines a light on important issues facing a minority group, but does nothing to ensure members of that group are compensated/helped. The perpetrator then gets acclaim for exposing societal truths while the group who's being affected by inequality is left to suffer. It's a lot like when someone asks you to write for a project they're working on, then offers you no compensation for your labor, citing you'll be paid in exposure. For more on this topic, I highly suggest reading Ashley J. Cooper's article "Hollywood Needs to Stop Stealing Trans Stories" on *The Establishment*.*

6. *Avoid creating tokens.* You can never have "too many" queer, female, or nonwhite characters. This kind of thinking is unhelpful and dehumanizing, since it presents underrepresented minorities as special interest groups whose stories would only have worth for the demographic they represent.

7. *It's okay for your minority characters to have flaws.* No one wants or expects you to make every queer character the pinnacle of moral goodness. What we DO want are queer characters with real, believable flaws that go beyond our sexuality and/or gender expression. Writers often shy away from imparting flaws onto their minority characters due to fear of accidentally stereotyping—but a perfect character isn't a human character, and we deserve to be human, too. A good way to check yourself is to question whether your character's flaws are directly related to their minority status. If yes, there's a good chance that character is stereotyped. This is

---

* Ashley J. Cooper, "Hollywood Needs to Stop Stealing Trans Stories," *The Establishment*, last modified July 3, 2017, https://theestablishment.co/hollywood -needs-to-stop-stealing-trans-stories-688e1c8b36cb.

another area where research is important, but empathy is equally crucial. Consider giving characters flaws that you possess, because you know how to write those struggles. The more research you do and more practice you have at writing outside your demographic, the more natural it will become. A word of caution though: no matter how much experience you gain, you'll never have the authority to speak for others. Always keep your mind open and remember that everyone deserves respect.

8. *Reversing a trope isn't always the right call.* This can be a great way to comment on how a demographic is portrayed, but be careful not to create equally reductive characters in pursuit of parody. A little depth goes a long way.

9. *Think intersectionally!* Everyone belongs to more than one demographic. For instance, I'm a mid-twenties, cat-loving, queer woman with an unabashed love of *Dragon Ball Z* and *The Silmarillion.* I'm also Caucasian, cis, an Army brat, and too many other things to name. Learn where overlap exists in your audience, and use it to your advantage. Maybe it's time to sprinkle a *Borderlands* reference into your mobile RTS.

10. *Consider adjacent demographics.* Once you've identified areas of overlap, think about how you can add subtle flourishes that encourage those demographics to play your game. Kids' cartoons are notorious for this; the creators know parents are watching, so they'll throw in a few jokes children won't understand in the hopes of entertaining this second demographic. If you're writing a children's game, those asides might increase the enjoyment of both parties, leading to more playtime. If you're creating a makeover game, consider adding a mode for fantasy/horror makeup. The players who enjoy the general idea of a makeover game still have fun, but you also allow new kinds of players to enjoy that genre. Just do me a favor—don't separate those modes on gender lines.

If you're ever in doubt about one of the above items, it's okay. Consider hiring a diversity consultant to help edit your narrative or, if you have the means, hire additional writing staff who are part of the demographic you're trying to portray.

Good, socially conscious writing isn't just better for your audience; it's good for your bottom line.

a test case

The case study we'll be looking at in this chapter is a PC/console title, but it does have several hallmarks of mobile gaming. It's *Battle Chef Brigade* (henceforth known as BCB, Trinket Studios, 2017), a match-3 game about cooking. Doesn't even sound like a PC/console title, does it?

Let's talk about that for a second. Why does BCB inherently sound like a mobile game, and what does that have to do with perceived demographics of mobile gamers? In the current climate of gaming elitism, mobile games are still largely considered casual, despite the enormous amount of time players spend on them. There's also the stereotype that most mobile gamers are women and that, indeed, those are the only games we play. When you combine that with the patriarchal notion that women are the core audience for anything domestic, you get the sense that BCB is a game aimed at women.

And you'd be right! I wrote BCB for everybody. When AAA companies say things like that, they generally mean "We wrote this game for white boys," and that's definitely not what I mean. I wrote this game for women and queer people and all other underrepresented groups. Our stories are universal stories, and they deserve recognition and respect. Though they're broken down into the more specific demographics in the following paragraphs, the team at Trinket Studios and I attempted to mirror the world as we know it to be—one of diversity.

When I started working on BCB, I didn't immediately think, "How can I reach our target demographic?" I find that approach to be too reductive and cynical. I *did* write BCB for everyone, but I also made sure to tailor my writing to the people I believed would be its biggest fans: anime geeks and foodies. While neither is a prototypical gaming demographic, BCB isn't a prototypical game.

Let's start with the anime geeks. I did very little upfront research on this demographic, simply because I've been a part of it since childhood. I even purposefully avoided watching cooking anime like *Shokugeki no Soma* to keep BCB's vision pure. Instead, years of junk-food-fueled *Toonami* nights came flowing through my fingers as I lead Mina and Thrash through the culinary competition of their lives.

Format and Fanfiction

While fanfiction has always been a part of all media, for me it's inextricably linked with anime. I'd written a few family plays in the mid-1990s, but it wasn't until I found the now defunct Anime Web Turnpike in 1999 that I decided I wanted to be a writer. Those early experiences are extremely pronounced in BCB. The most notable are Mina's stutters. Fanfiction is, by its definition, an amateur practice, so writers aren't bound by strict grammatical guidelines. This freedom allows for experimentation with format that is unparalleled in other mediums, and gives readers a more personalized experience. Since the majority of anime fans have at least a passing familiarity with fanfiction, I wanted to visually reference that style with Mina's signature tilde (see below).

Mina's nervous excitement is palpable as she registers for the Proving Tournament. Screenshot from *Battle Chef Brigade*. Developed by Trinket Studios and is protected by United States and international copyright law. © Trinket Studios, Inc.

It's hardly a dramatic change from a hyphen, but it conveys personality and sets Mina's speech visually apart from other characters. A player can infer from the squiggle that Mina is nervous and unsure of herself even before reading her actual dialogue. Thorn, the depressed combat instructor, also has an unconventional affectation. Her boredom and near-constant hangover cause her to speak slowly, a trait visually reinforced by large spaces between her sentences. These things are subtle—most players won't even think about them, but for you, as a narrative designer, it's important to keep visual design in mind. Since games are primarily designed to be played and not read (unless you're playing a visual novel or other narrative-heavy genre), any extra characterization you can sneak into your text is critical. (For more on dialogue and visual design, see Chapter 5, "More Than Pretty Words: Functional Dialogue.")

Thorn loves the hunt. You, on the other hand, are a headache. Screenshot from *Battle Chef Brigade*. Developed by Trinket Studios and is protected by United States and international copyright law. © Trinket Studios, Inc.

In addition to BCB's visual design, many of the characters' personalities are based on tropes commonly found in anime: Mina as the wide-eyed protagonist, Thrash as the jolly friend, Kirin as the intellectual wallflower, Ziggy as the mysterious traveler from another plane. The list goes on. Though none of them fully fall into these tropes, Eric Huang (Trinket Studios' Creative Director) and I intentionally played off them to make the BCB cast feel instantly familiar. But wait—didn't I just spend a large section of this chapter vigorously cautioning *against* the use of tropes? There are a couple differences here: these tropes have nothing to do with intrinsic qualities like race or gender, and the BCB cast are still fully realized characters and transcend the tropes on which they're based.

Even the way the characters interact is partially based upon anime/fanfiction roots. Eric and I made a conscious decision not to put many canon romantic partnerships in the game, allowing players to explore shipping possibilities. For those not familiar, "shipping" refers to the act of a fan placing characters into romantic relationships; generally the characters are not together within the main story, though they can be. This choice sprang from my immediate need to write about BCB's characters the moment I saw them. Even before I was hired as the game's narrative designer, I was so inspired by Eric's designs that I spent my free time dreaming up themed restaurants the cast might open. I'm fairly certain other writers will feel the same way, so I intentionally wove multiple shipping options into the game. ShivxKirin 4 life!!

Delicious Research and Foodie Family

The foodie demographic didn't come quite as naturally to me. I'd seen a few competitive cooking shows back in my cable days, but they never really spoke to me. That is, until I started working on BCB. I watched hours of competitive cooking shows, sprinkling *Iron Chef* in sparingly—Chairman Kamin would need to find his voice apart from Chairman Kaga, after all. I began going to restaurants and really reading my menus, always talking to knowledgeable wait staff and chefs who had the time. At home I cooked new recipes, meditated on holiday meals past, and tried to think about all the reasons people make food for each other. Research doesn't have to be boring; make it your own! It was completely indispensable when I sat down to write hundreds of lines of judge dialogue.

The research opened up a whole new realm of character possibilities previously unconsidered; once I understood why chefs created food for others, I began ascribing those traits to our cast. I also came to understand that food is both universal and intimate. The bonds created from this shared experience of caregiving and appreciation are undeniably appealing for those who love food. That became a central focus of every interaction the player has with BCB's cast. All dialogue should reveal character, but this felt different: I wanted to mirror the experience a diner has with a chef. This was best achieved through Thrash, a playable Orc nicknamed The Benevolent Berserker. Thrash's desire to cook stems directly from his desire to give back to his family and culture, and he's not shy about sharing those values with the player.

this is all great, but my limit is 500 words

Not all games can or should have large, sweeping narratives with ample space for character development. How, then, do you take the lessons from previous sections and apply them? It can be challenging, but not nearly impossible.

Let's look at Playrix Games's *Gardenscapes* (2016) opening as an example. For a mobile match-3, the writers knew they had very little time to present the game's story upfront. A key theme throughout all mobile demographics is the assumption that player fatigue won't allow for more than a few seconds of exposition. Still, the writers manage to pack an impressive amount of world and character building into about 40 seconds worth of VO:

1. Explains what you're doing—going to your great uncle's old estate.
2. Explains why you're doing it—you want to get away from your busy, city life.
3. Conveys the setting—your great uncle probably couldn't manage an estate that large in his old age.
4. Tells the player who they are—uses vague descriptors that fit most people in order to have the broadest appeal.
5. Introduces the main character—Austin's your butler, and he'll be tutorializing everything for you.

The game goes on to do plenty of worldbuilding, but all the player's basic narrative needs are accomplished upfront. Even if there was no narrative justification for the rest of the game, you'd understand that you're matching tiles to improve your new home. They've also done something similar to BCB, where they use the mild-mannered butler trope to introduce Austin but don't constrain him to it. The more the player learns about him, the more he is revealed to be a complex and interesting character. While this is done throughout the game, signs that he's a fully realized character pop up within the first minute of gameplay.

demographics vs. reality: when your boss doesn't care

So far, we've assumed that you have creative control over the game you're writing, but what happens when that isn't true? While demographics can be a useful tool for understanding your audience, they can also be used as an excuse to make questionable creative decisions.

Take a few examples from my career. I once worked on a game where a parody of a famous Egyptian ruler was whitewashed. During the development process, I advocated for the character's skin color to be changed in order to match the historical figure better. Unfortunately, my arguments were ignored. When it came time for me to adjust the character's in-game bio, I made a simple narrative change instead:

make this character an oblivious white person in a Halloween costume and REALLY make fun of their lack of empathy and cultural acumen. The bio got reverted to its original state and the character went into the game unaltered.

Another game I worked on contained a very pointed rape joke aimed at a minor. As in the previous scenario, I argued for this to be taken out throughout our development process. Nearly the entire team working on the game agreed that it was offensive and needed to be removed. This time, I wasn't simply told no; I was punished for speaking up. Over a year later, the joke was hurriedly removed in a patch after that IP's creative team expressed concern over it.

Why weren't these items addressed? To the ones making those decisions, the answer was simple: our demographic didn't care about these kinds of issues. It didn't matter that the subject matter was uncreative, jarring, and added nothing to these games. It didn't matter that our demographic was based on foregone conclusions rather than data, and it certainly didn't matter that this presumed demographic received no benefit from the inclusion of these things.

So, what do you do as a writer in this scenario? First and foremost, practice self-care. I know what you're thinking: this is a book about writing, not a self-help guide! Trust me, a breathing exercise here and a good night sleep there is critical for any writer. This is especially true when your working life becomes creatively contentious.

Once you've rested a bit, it's time for action. The number one thing you can do as a writer on a poor creative team is mitigate bad decisions. Use your knowledge of demographics to your advantage. Here are a few thought experiments:

Your team decides to include only one Asian character in an upcoming match-3 game. When the character artist gives you their design, you wince: the character is inexplicably wearing a gi and has a Fu Manchu beard to rival any Klingon warrior. The other proposed characters are wearing regular street clothes, and the game itself has no explicit tie to martial arts. What do you do?

1. *Talk to the artist.* This can be awkward since 9 times out of 10, the person you're talking to has unintentionally violated one of our ground rules above. Explain to them why you're concerned and suggest they do a little research of their own. Hopefully they listen, if not...

2. *Talk to the art director/creative lead.* It's even better if you can show the art to other members of your team and get them

to join you. Express your concern for alienating Asian players, particularly if you plan to localize and launch the game
in Asia. When talking to management, always try to couple
your qualitative argument with a quantitative one; they're in
business to make money, and potentially losing business over
consumer outcry is not the way to do that. Hopefully, they
listen, if not...

3. *Continue to make noise about it.* Don't stop until the game is
launched. Hopefully someone will listen to you before then, if
not...

4. *The pen really can be mightier than the sword.* You can't help
what your coworker has done, but you can try your best to do
right by your audience anyway. A lazier writer might create
a biography and dialogue for this character that reference a
strict upbringing and love for kung fu (joke's on them—it's a
karate gi), but not you. You'll mention their passion for making realistic gingerbread houses.

5. *Don't stop with the problematic character; get the others
involved.* Have one character ask the aspiring breadchitect
(I know how forced that is, okay?) why he's dressed like that.
Maybe he's agreed to be part of a community theatre production on the dangers of stereotypes. Maybe those are just his
pajamas.

6. *Once you've used every weapon in your keyboard arsenal, go
get some sleep.* If an issue has escalated this much, there are
plenty more on the horizon. Take care of yourself, so you're
ready to fight when the next comes along.

a thought experiment

Even writing this chapter required me to consider audience demographics. Should I gear my writing toward aspiring writers or those
with professional experience? If my explanations contained too much
jargon, they wouldn't be approachable for the former. On the other
hand, if I offered no new insights or spoke too simply, the latter
would find this whole chapter boring. Ultimately, I decided to cater
to the aspiring demographic while still keeping the seasoned demographic in mind. This decision helped me decide how to proceed with

everything from the tone of what you're reading to its layout. Let's take a look:

Tone: Conversational. Writing is supposed to be fun and inclusive; I wanted to give readers a sense of myself, so they might find the material more approachable. At the same time, small doses of humor (hopefully) keep those with a plethora of professional writing experience more engaged through the easier portions.

Diction: Again, avoiding jargon and placing a premium on readability. A layman can pick up this chapter and learn new keywords, but isn't overwhelmed with unfamiliar vocabulary. A master can breeze through it and pick up a few new tricks for their creative arsenal.

Subject matter: A 60/40 split between beginner and advanced concepts.

Content distribution: Starts with the basics then slowly moves into more advanced subject matter. From golden rules to how you pare all this information down into an endless runner's tutorial. This ascent includes a shift from presuming the narrative designer as solo creative to a member of a larger team. The aspiring-writer demographic likely works alone, but still wants advice for later in their careers. Seasoned writers are much more likely to work in a group setting, or have done so in the past.

tools for you

Sadly, we've reached the end of this meditation on demographics, but consider these exercises as your parting gift.

1. Have you researched the demographic(s) you hope to reach with your game?
2. Have you created detailed character biographies for all major characters?
3. Are these bios influencing the way you approach the design of each characters' speech?
4. Have you thought about ways to visually represent your characters' personalities through text?

5. Could any of the elements of your narrative design be perceived as stereotypical and/or offensive?

6. If you're not a member of the demographic you're writing for, have you asked members of that demographic to provide feedback on your game's narrative design?

7. If you're still concerned and have the means, have you hired a diversity consultant?

8. If you've drawn inspiration/information from members of the demographic you're writing for, have those individuals been properly cited and/or compensated?

9. Is your work devoid of token characters?

10. Do your characters have flaws that are appropriate for them as individuals?

11. Have you considered how players within your target demographic will view your game?

12. Have you considered how players outside your target demographic will view your game?

13. Have you thought about how adjacent demographics could influence your game?

14. Have you seen any aspects of the game that could be stereotypical/offensive?

15. Have you raised any creative issues to your game's creative lead?

how the folk tale got its leopard
writing for educational games

Erin Hoffman-John

contents

introduction to educational games

Educational videogames have been around nearly as long as videogames themselves but, in recent years, our language for understanding their unique value proposition to learners, teachers, and parents has increased significantly. It's therefore worth starting any conversation on videogames and education with a recap on why videogames provide special learning opportunities that are enticing new developers to enter the field.

Games are unique vehicles for educational content for a few reasons:

- *Personalized learning*: every student is an individual, and yet most formal education takes place at low-ratio scales (1 teacher to 20–30 students); videogames have a 1:1 relationship between the learner and the learning material and, unlike static materials, they dynamically adapt to the performance of the learner: in educational circles, this is known as "personalized learning";
- *Failing forward*: failure is a key to how we learn, and yet most traditional learning environments have created such high-stakes environments that learners don't feel that it's safe to fail. In a game, it's always safe to fail and try again—that's what an "extra life" is all about; and
- *Modern media language*: videogames are a native part of the media space of modern kids, and so educational content through the videogame medium reaches kids on a level that they find approachable, familiar, and modern.

These are just a few reasons that address educational videogames on a high level. When it comes to specific subjects, videogames have particular leverage because of other intrinsic qualities:

- *Videogames are dynamic*: concepts such as ratios in math, "sigma" combinations in calculus, empathy in English language arts, and state change in chemistry all benefit from being experienced in "moving" media that the player controls because they all involve change over time;

- *Videogames are interactive*: any experience in which perspective-taking enhances learning—such as roleplaying perspectives in civics or managing a fictional store in economics—is particularly strong in a videogame because all videogame experiences are first person and directly experiential; and

- *Videogames are patient*: a game, unlike a person, possesses infinite patience, and so a skill that requires a high degree of repetition (such as multiplication or spelling) can be more easily experienced in a videogame.

While many early developers of educational videogames suspected all of the above in the early days of this kind of content, our ability to tightly articulate the strengths and weaknesses of videogames for education allows us a much higher degree of precision in our choices with regard to educational videogame content than we have ever had before. More frictionless high-quality content generation tools also dramatically enhance the capability of educational games, which often are built with lower budgets than for-profit games.

What's Special about mobile?

As you will have read already, the interaction affordances of mobile games are unique in the world of games. That is to say: the physical actions you take to play a mobile game—what the physical platform affords or invites you to do—are unlike those of any other platform. When designing for a unique environment, it's important to always keep these immutable physical properties in mind:

- *Touchscreens!*: instead of being separated from the game by a mouse, keyboard, or controller, you directly touch the art;

- *Screen size*: usually, mobile devices have smaller screens than other gaming platforms, though the real bugbear with mobile is that you may be designing for several different screen sizes simultaneously;

- *Probable environment*: players interact with mobile platforms in different circumstances than they do personal computers or gaming-specific consoles—you can't assume that you'll have their undivided attention;

- *Software keyboards*: you can communicate with players by having them input text, but that affordance can be limited and clunky;
- *Intermittent Internet*: because of the shifting locale of mobile devices, you can be pretty sure your players are going to be accessing games without Wi-Fi access some of the time; and
- *Push notifications*: the ubiquity and mobility of mobile devices aren't just a limitation, though being able to hide away and then later tap your players on the shoulder when they aren't even necessarily thinking of your game is a unique design affordance with particular story leverage.

All of these affordances combine to inflect the learning experience in a few ways:

- *Wide age demographics*: the audience that you could be trying to teach through your game varies in age from 0 to 110 (people live a long time these days!)—all ages have access to mobile phones;
- *The buyer is (probably) not the player*: universally with games for youth or children, but especially in the case of mobile devices, educational games are almost never purchased by the person who will be consuming them—they are gifted (or pushed!) on younger players by parents and relatives;
- *Wide socioeconomic demographics*: particularly if you are deploying to Android devices, you'll experience not just wide age and cultural demographics, but also wide socioeconomic demographics—parent-buyers who have radically differ-ent goals and preferences with regard to their educational software—which means tightly targeting the socioeconomic demographic of your purchaser is crucial; and
- *Challenging financial models*: most mobile games still operate on a "sample" basis, with "lite" editions of mobile games offered for free and loaded with upsell messaging to the paid app.

These dynamics may not seem directly related to your learning expe-rience, or to your writing-for-learning experience, but they are a critical context in which to understand your goals and your constraint space.

With that context established, we can move on to design principles specific to writing for educational games.

principles

Learning as Storytelling

When considering the role of writing and storytelling in educational content, it's important to remember that language is central to our human experience of learning itself, and learning is key to our survival as a species. Our ability to speak to one another and bridge gaps in experience gave us immortality as a species, and the ability to adapt and evolve beyond our biology. Once we could speak and transfer knowledge between ourselves—to learn without requiring first-hand experience—we then developed storytelling to compress this learning and make it more efficient and more memorable.

Our universal human sense for "how a story should go" is directly connected to this learning process. Storytelling techniques, such as "inevitable surprise," "reversal," "foreshadowing," "dramatic reveals," "call to adventure," "escalation," and "crisis," all connect conceptually to learning: all of these concern the revelation of information to the audience through the plot, which is to say, what the audience is learning about the story as it progresses. When we learn things through stories that change the way we think about the world—and especially change how we think the world works—that is a transformative experience. And we often have these transformative experiences through storytelling, which is why we study theme and meaning in the analysis of literary works.

Characterization is another compression technique that ultimately functions to transfer information to the audience. The protagonist of a story exists to personify certain characteristics and world beliefs. Those beliefs then come into conflict with the world as it really is through the plot. Secondary characters represent aspects of that world, especially where it conflicts with the perspective of the protagonist. The resolution of this conflict is a learning experience for both the protagonist and the audience; we learn along with them.

In designing Zodiac Flynn, the central character for *Mars Generation One: Argubot Academy* (GlassLab, Inc., 2014), I wanted to evoke the power fantasy of Japanese roleplaying games I had loved as a kid, synthesized with a Golden Age science-fiction sense of adventure. Zodiac therefore was new on the scene at Argubot Academy, but feisty, confident, and bold. I allowed the player to shape Zodiac's characterization by choosing dialogue that was often either assertive or ameliorating but, by setting the range of those choices, I channeled them into a role that was analytical, thoughtful, and direct—characteristics that were desirable traits in effective conflict mediators. At the same time, Zodiac and the other kids in the academy were wacky and fun-loving—and their robot dog, S.A.M. (Social Animal Machine), was my mechanism to inject a dry humor into the narrative that offered opportunities for double-encoding (themes that resonate one way with kids and a second way with adults, both of which are intentional).

Screenshot from *Mars Generation One: Argubot Academy.* Developed/published by GlassLab and is protected by United States and international copyright law. © GlassLab

Inevitable Surprise and Emergence

One of the most crucial concepts at the intersection of storytelling, games, and learning is what the storytelling world calls *inevitable surprise*. This concept captures the way in which a well-crafted story leads the reader to a moment of genuine surprise, but the immediate reflection following that surprise is "of course!" or "how did I miss that?!" The surprise feels inevitable once it has been revealed; there could be no other answer, and yet it is delightful and unexpected.

In videogame design, we have a parallel concept specific to the design of complex systems called *emergence*. Sharing a Latin root with *emergency*, emergence has the built-in idea that it produces unexpected consequences. If you saw it coming, you would have done something about it, and so it doesn't become an emergency. Emergencies emerge out of complex situations with many interrelated parts—kind of the way a surprising result can pop out of a complex game of *SimCity*. The key to these moments of surprise in complex system-based games, however, is that the player 1) understands and 2) accepts the unexpected result. The player should have that same inevitable surprise feeling of "of course!" that we experience in the reveal scene of a great mystery novel.

What's happening in both of these instances is, distinctly, learning. The inevitable surprise reveals to us the complexity that we did not consider, perceive, or understand. Absorbing that new logic into our world model causes us to grow. This is learning, and it is why learning is the sprawling root system of the organisms we call storytelling and game design.

Because storytelling for educational purposes taps into all of these potential avenues for language-based expression and storytelling that reaches into the creative space beyond language, the subject of writing and storytelling for educational purposes is phenomenally broad and deep—full of complexity and potential. Its study could be a lifelong one but, for these purposes, it's best to again keep in mind the possibility space while considering some specific guidelines.

In the meantime, consider your own learning-through-language experiences, or even your most moving "nonlearning" storytelling experiences. In your favorite books, movies, or plays, what did you not know before experiencing those stories? What might you have stealthily learned while thinking you were just enjoying yourself?

Knowing Your Audience for Educational Games

As we've discussed with respect to platform, having a very precise sense of who your audience is—and, again, with a learning mobile game, it's probably two audiences: the purchasing audience and the playing audience—is crucial.

In an entertainment game such as *Super Mario Bros.*, the playing audience can be extremely broad. Kids as young as four or five can play the game, along with middle schoolers, high schoolers, and adults. The pleasure of the visual and sound feedback is fairly universal, as is the enjoyment of mastering the physics-based challenges of this well-scaffolded linear franchise.

By contrast, an effective learning game is laser specific. While *Mario* can be enjoyable to play even if mastered (though admittedly it is less fun when truly completely familiar), a learning game isolates specific kinds of usually more abstract learning that, once assimilated, becomes much less interesting. This, too, is deeply instinctive; once we have incorporated learning into our world model, our brains are not very motivated to repeat it because they are hungry for new learning.

This means that a very precise picture of one's audience when designing a learning game is critically important. This is true of all learning content, but it is especially true of learning games because a given human developmental phase of learning is usually paired with some aspect of physical development. If you design a color exploration game that involves touching and dragging, the content may be appropriate for a one-year-old who lacks the motor control to touch and drag, so your game winds up in a no-man's-land without any audience at all. This gap between learning content and interaction affordance can be thought of as a kind of dissonance, similar to *ludonarrative dissonance* (when the feelings evoked by a game's mechanics are at odds with the feelings evoked by its story), and it is particularly dangerous to learning games.

It is also true that the younger one aims in audience, the more precise that content and affordance target becomes. You can safely assume a number of things about a five-year-old in terms of their ability to hold a handheld device, touch specific places, swipe, drag—whereas those assumptions become much more fragile for two-year-olds or three-year-olds. This creates another conundrum: learning content for these younger ages is much clearer and well understood, but their physical capabilities limit them from many kinds of game mechanics; older kids are more physically capable and generally more engaged by games, but matching their more complex learning content to game mechanics is a much more challenging and less well-understood space.

One important concept to bear in mind when writing for educational mobile games particularly pertaining to story is Lexile level. The specificity that applies to game audiences for physical interactions also applies to language. English language educators have identified various dimensions of language—such as vocabulary, sentence length, grammatical complexity, and more—that make a given piece of text more or less challenging to read. Tools such as Lexile.com allow you to copy and paste passages of your game's text into the site and receive back a measurement of the text's Lexile level. Checking text against this kind of tool frequently can be a good way of homing in on exactly the right level of complexity in your writing. And, importantly, you should target that audience before beginning work on the game and familiarize yourself with the boundaries for writing to that grade level.

When crafting the script for *Mars Generation One*—an adventure game that ultimately contained over 40,000 words of character dialogue—I continuously ran the entire script through the Lexile

Analyzer to make sure I was hitting my reading age targets through-out development.

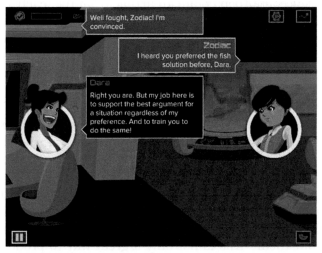

Screenshot from *Mars Generation One: Argubot Academy*. Developed/published by GlassLab and is protected by United States and international copyright law. © GlassLab

Integrating with Pedagogy

When writing for an educational game, or creating any kind of content intended to be experienced in schools, integrating with pedagogy—which is to say supporting your game with classroom materials and support for teachers who may want to use it—is critical. At a minimum, consider some basic constraints from the teacher-as-user perspective:

- *Classes are short*: realistically, your game must be experienced in 15-minute chunks, since a given 30-minute class needs time for "warm up," device distribution, and cleanup;
- *Many students use the same device*: so user management and save states must be designed accordingly; and
- *Teachers are busy*: simple, straightforward setup instructions along with a set of suggestions for how to play the game and troubleshoot are crucial, along with a bullet-point list of what standards your game addresses.

A good reference point for how a creative work can slot into a classroom is the discussion guide you often find at the end of middle-grade fiction novels. These discussion templates give teachers a perfect "jumping off" point for homework, essays, or classroom discussions without being heavily prescriptive. They're also useful in thinking about the kind of experience teachers often want; getting a student to reflect on their experience and then create an artifact that the teacher can evaluate (an essay, for instance) is the "learning loop" teachers are looking for. What's notable from a writing perspective is that these discussion guides are authored pieces of written content in and of themselves. Often, they're written by curriculum designers, but you as a content creator can draft them as you develop the core game.

Something you may find is that one of the best ways of integrating story into your learning game is to create classroom materials that expand on the world of your story. In this way, the best learning game experiences are not just contained within the game, but also comprise a holistic learning experience.

Creativity is an especially important lever in supplementing a learning game with classroom materials. Have students draw pictures of characters in your game or write short stories or journal entries about them—this is not only a great way to produce a measurable artifact for a teacher, but also a way to more deeply engage the learner with your work and your game world.

Working with Learning Game Designers

In the best circumstances, making a learning game involves adding at least one, and possibly two, new disciplines to the already multidisciplinary process of making a videogame: learning designers and assessment designers.

Learning designers—sometimes called curriculum designers—come from a variety of backgrounds, but often they have some kind of upper-level teaching degree (for example, a master's degree in education) and some practical teaching experience. One program that is yielding a large number of learning designers in the tech space is Teach for America, a program that recruits graduates from top-tier colleges to teach for two years in high-need areas. These program graduates go on to serve a variety of functions in the civic and education space: some continue to teach, others move into administration, and still more into politics and also into technology. What they have in common is the combination of boots-on-the-ground teaching experience with a desire to attempt to address education on a larger scale.

As with the introduction of any new discipline, advanced collaboration is required in integrating the expertise of learning designers into the process. This is especially true for disciplines related to a game's design, which learning design must inevitably be. Entire books could be written about the construction of this collaboration. Because it is fundamentally a codesign process (if it's being done well), the success of this collaborative relationship is absolutely instrumental in creating games that are both educational and engaging. Mutual respect is crucial. The learning designer must respect that an educational game that isn't fun is a failure. The game creator must respect that an educational game that doesn't teach—or teaches misconceptions, which is the more common flaw—is a failure.

This double veto is central to the creation of effective, engaging educational games, and is also what makes the process of collaboration between learning designers and game creators so challenging. The team must have the fortitude to iterate and iterate and iterate until a solution is found that meets the criteria for engagement and learning. Therefore, the best advice is the simplest and the hardest: maintain respect, and maintain your endurance for iteration. Be prepared to learn from each other every day.

Finally, the following sections will explore some of the complexities specific to writing for certain learning subjects.

types of educational games

Writing for Games about the Humanities

With today's focus on games for STEM (science, technology, engineering, and math), it's easy to forget that videogames have tremendous leverage assisting with the process of learning to read, and—equally important—learning to love reading.

The same principles that make videogames great for learning broadly also apply to the experience of learning language arts. Games provide personalized experiences—a second-person adventure in which every kid is the hero. Games provide agency—fictional environments where choices matter, which is especially important for exploring subjects such as civic responsibility, historical empathy (what did they do? why did they do it? would you have done the same thing?), and philosophy (what are the rules for how we should live?). In addition, because games are "lean forward" experiences that require interaction to progress the story, they are engaging and simultaneously instant measurements of a student's progress. With a "lean back" experience, such as a book or a movie, it's impossible to know whether a student has been paying attention to the story; with a game, you know how much interaction has taken place because the game won't progress without it.

Because of this "lean forward" requirement, games are uniquely suited to a skill called *close reading*, which is one of the holy grails of language education. Games such as *Pokémon* and *Phoenix Wright* require the player to pay close attention to the text displayed in the game. The text is what provides the player with winning strategies, which are quite difficult to discover randomly. Because of this, success in the game is gated by literacy, and so the performance on a given level or boss battle, for example, is an illustration of the player's ability to read. This is probably the single greatest advantage a game for learning reading has over linear media experiences: the mechanics of the game can inspire young players to pay close attention to the words, and more importantly, the meaning of specific words, in order to achieve success in the game. This process of reading carefully to decipher meaning is one of the most central skills in language learning.

When we tested *Mars Generation One*, we were especially gratified when our teacher partners expressed astonished pleasure at how students would actually slow each other down to closely read the game's dialogue. Because success in the game depended upon picking up facts from the environment and understanding those facts (physical "evidence" on chips distributed around the game), carefully reading each piece of evidence was fundamental in successfully winning an argubot battle.

Screenshot from *Mars Generation One: Argubot Academy*. Developed/published by GlassLab and is protected by United States and international copyright law. © GlassLab

Writing for Games about Math

You might not think of writing to be something you primarily consider for math games, but if you think for a moment about the infamous frustrating nonsense that we associate with the "word problem," you have experienced why there is in fact a great and drastic need for writing and storytelling in the instruction of math.

Because much of math instruction concerns the manipulation of abstracts, the ability to situate a "problem" (and, to a certain extent, you can see the absence of symbolic wordcrafting in that we refer to math as associated with problems) in an imaginary environment is extremely powerful. It allows us to tap into other parts of our brain and leverage creative thinking in mapping an unfamiliar knowledge space. It also has the power to make an abstract problem far more engaging.

James Paul Gee (whose work is a must-study for those interested in educational games) describes one of the greatest powers of educational videogames as their potential to create situated context and deliver situated meaning.

Consider a challenge of the average classroom. You, as a teacher, are in front of 20–30 students who may come from very diverse backgrounds. Especially if you're teaching in a low-income environment, those backgrounds can vary widely indeed. Kids may or may not have spent much time outdoors. They might or might not have watched the same television shows. The space of their experience is broad and varied.

A shared experience directly connected to classroom material provides situated context. It provides a common experience that the teacher absolutely knows the whole class shares. This gives the teacher a bridge of metaphors to the student, and a way of speaking to all of them at once.

This advantage holds particular leverage in math. By teaching fractions with pizza or ratios with feeding animals, we create a metaphor space that allows students to connect to lived experiences. They'll understand more, more deeply, and faster because they can leverage the full-learning capabilities of their experience-oriented brain against these abstract problems.

These choices are writing and storytelling choices. The right metaphor is crucial, and sussing that out requires both creativity and collaboration with your subject-matter experts. When we don't have the right metaphors—either because they're a mismatch for the material or because they're boring or nonsensical—we get saddled with bad word problems that exacerbate the friction in learning these skills rather than smoothing it.

Writing for Games about Science

Similar to math, writing is not the first discipline that comes to mind in thinking of games about science but, in terms of creating situated context, storytelling is crucial. Furthermore, modern advances in science education identify science literacy as a core skill in science, emphasizing the role that language arts have in a science education. Because the practice of science broadly involves reasoning that is usually expressed in the form of language, the process of hypothesizing, then validating that hypothesis (or failing to do so), which is at the core of all science, relies on literacy skills. Modern practicing science organizations, such as NASA, also understand that many of the communicative skills involved in the development of language arts—especially empathy, collaboration, and communication—are also necessary in the scientific world.

Beyond the role of literacy, the practice of science, language, and many skills associated with storytelling—such as characterization and worldbuilding—amplifies the creation of a believable world that can sufficiently immerse and engage students in such a way as to prime them for science learning. Concepts of "cause and effect" or pattern recognition can be dry and obtuse or vibrant and addictive, depending on the context in which they are presented. The use of language to create immersive worlds thus can be quite fundamental to creating compelling science content in videogames.

Finally, modern science education also recognizes an intersecting space between science and the humanities in fields such as sustainability studies, environmental science, and human behavioral change. The practice of these growing areas of modern science involves *stakeholder theory*—a kind of perspective taking that emphasizes not just the rational correctness of a solution, but also its sufficiency to the needs of involved stakeholders—which in turn brings in humanities' skills, such as communication and collaboration in the process of defining stakeholder criteria and predicting human behavior.

Considering all of these factors, it should be clear how the writing and the creation of believable characters become extremely important in the delivery of engaging science games. Great science games create worlds, populate them with vivid characters, and provide just the right context to illuminate the reasoning behind a given science concept. Should the game splash about in water? Crash together rocks? Measure slimy nematodes? You, as a writer, and especially if you are the kind to thoughtfully construct settings for stories, are uniquely equipped to make these decisions.

In *Mars Generation One*, we worked with our collaborators at NASA to find the most fascinating, dramatic problems that future pioneers would have to solve in order for humans to live on the red planet. We fused argumentation with the science by isolating problems that don't have clear right or wrong answers, and then presenting evidence from both sides. The result was a game world that left students talking long after the game itself about, for instance, what sort of food we should eat on Mars, or whether robots deserve to be treated with compassion.

Screenshot from *Mars Generation One: Argubot Academy*. Developed/published by GlassLab and is protected by United States and international copyright law. © GlassLab

Writing for Games about Social Skills

One of the newest and most in-demand fields for learning games are those games that teach SEL: social and emotional learning. CASEL (the Collaborative for Academic, Social, and Emotional Learning), the leading organization for SEL, defines it this way: "Social and emotional learning (SEL) is the process through which children and adults acquire and effectively apply the knowledge, attitudes, and skills necessary to understand and manage emotions, set and achieve positive goals, feel and show empathy for others, establish and maintain positive relationships, and make responsible decisions."*

A growing area in education, SEL competencies, such as active listening, self-awareness, teamwork, ethical responsibility, and problem-solving, are particularly suited to learning through character-based story experiences where the player has agency—which is to say, humanities-heavy learning games. Many techniques from role-playing games enhance lessons for social and emotional learning. Psychology techniques that inform the creation of believable characters create fertile ground for students to experiment safely with high-stakes social interactions.

When writing for SEL games, it's important to do one's own homework in the creation of careful characters that avoid stereotypes, especially culturally harmful stereotypes.† Furthermore, as SEL is still a growing field, we often have a tendency to assume expertise that we don't have. The agency, consequential nature, and safe experimentation spaces afforded by videogames give them great leverage in teaching SEL skills, and effective writing is crucial in the delivery of well-rounded characters from which the player can learn—provided that developers approach SEL with their own growth mindset firmly in place.

conclusion

These brief sections provide an overview of subject-specific writing for videogames. Each subject could be a chapter unto itself, so approach them with thoughtfulness, research, and attention to your subject-matter experts. In general, when embarking on writing for a specific learning subject, it can be useful to explore effective, informal nonfiction on that subject, augmented by fiction that uses the subject as its setting. By triangulating between these sources, you should be able to develop a general sense for the conventions of the field. Naturally, practicing subject-matter experts are great resources too, but remember that, being highly versed in their subject, they likely have forgotten the path they took to reach their expertise.

---

* "What Is SEL?," CASEL.org, accessed February 5, 2018. https://casel.org/what-is-sel/.

† For more on avoiding stereotypes, please see Chapter 7, "To Each Their Own: Writing for Demographics."

I like to ask subject-matter experts, "If you could teach an Nth grader just one thing about your subject, what would it be?" Regardless of whether you like their answer or not, they often find it a satisfyingly challenging question to answer.

quick tips

Now that you have a sense of the landscape of writing for educational games, we'll close with some quick tips for the creation of educational games in general.

Find a subject matter expert who finds their subject beautiful. This isn't necessarily the subject matter expert who holds the most mastery. It's the one that's a little creative and maybe a bit of a pariah because of it. Oliver Sacks for neuroscience, Carl Sagan for astrophysics. Their ability to bridge to imaginative worlds can contain hints for you.

Be humble, but persistent. Working with educational institutions and education experts can be exhausting and frustrating.

Maintaining a humble approach (often by reminding yourself that there are reasons for often labyrinthine institutional systems, or at least the history that created them) is critical in keeping collaboration alive, but you have to strike a balance in knowing when not to take "no" for an answer—that's the persistence.

Don't assume that you understand the problems pace of getting games into classrooms. When talking to subject-matter experts—and especially teachers—listen more than you talk.

Find and cherish teachers who are wizards with students. You will know this when you see it.

Talk to teachers. Often. If you're making a game for classrooms and you aren't in a classroom at least once a week, you are going to steer wildly off course and not even know it.

Don't underestimate kids. They understand far more than we often think they do, and their pains are as sophisticated as ours. Connect with that pain—which may mean connecting with your own childhood—and let it guide you to novel solutions that genuinely relieve it.

when writing for educational games...

- Decide, or get alignment on, your pedagogical approach—the way that you'll be teaching the subject, and why.
- Carefully target the audience that you are writing for, and identify their Lexile level.
- Use a Lexile leveling tool (such as the Lexile Analyzer) to measure your work as you go.
    - Remember that the short sentence style that is generally more effective in games tends to reduce Lexile level, so you may have to adjust it upward (assume that a Lexile level of 4 might be 5 if you adjust for short UI sentences).
- Think about the narrative progression inherent in attaining the skill you are teaching.
    - What "boss" represents the transition between ignorance and enlightenment in this skill?
    - What escalating difficulty can lend drama to your player experience, and how can you amplify that with storytelling?
    - What story can you tell about the sequence of subskills in the skill?
- Consider how you can start with a misconception about the skill and use characters and narrative to transform that misconception through moments of surprise into insight.
- Remember that all great learning is amplified by story: progression, conflict, rounded characters, stakes. Create believable, serious problems for your characters, and solve them with the skill you're teaching.
- Remember that the root of all meaningful learning is the question "Why?" Why is this skill important? What will happen if a person doesn't have it? Use these questions to guide yourself into naturally aligned drama.

Go forth, and be excellent! It's a tough space, but the learners want you there, and the sky is big, blue, and open.

playing with values
branding games

Toiya Kristen Finley, PhD

contents

There are all kinds of brands. Some brands include Coca Cola, Motorola, and DC Entertainment. While there are games licensed by brands like DC Entertainment and Marvel, we'll focus on working with licenses in Chapter 10, "The Continued Adventures: Writing for Licensed Mobile Games." These games are based on established intellectual property (IP) and take place in the IP's universes. The universes—including their worldbuilding, histories/events, and characters—serve as the foundations of these licensed games. This chapter focuses specifically on incorporating brands, without established, fictional universes, that are built around particular products, services, or philosophies. A brand is not just a product or service, but it is also the shaping of how consumers think and feel about that product or service. Therefore, brands use their games to engender in players' positive beliefs about their offerings and/or philosophies.

Some brands may work exclusively with a marketing or advertising agency to develop their games, but those agencies may subcontract a studio or narrative designer/game writer to assist, or the brand may hire a studio and work with it directly. If you find yourself tasked with coming up with the game's narrative design and story delivery, there are a few important things to understand about brands and branding games.

First, *branding isn't marketing*. Branding is about the values, principles, or philosophy behind an offering, whether it's a service or product:

> [Branding] is communication of characteristics, values, and attributes that clarify what this particular brand is and is not.
>
> A brand will help encourage someone to buy a product, and it directly supports whatever sales or marketing activities are in play, but the brand does not explicitly say "buy me." Instead, it says, "This is what I am. This is why I exist. If you agree, if you like me, you can buy me, support me, and recommend me to your friends."*

Branding isn't product placement. Booing and hissing are common reactions players have to product placement in videogames, especially when it's blatant. The essence of the brand is integral to the game's design and content. It not only appears in the game, but it also informs everything in it.

---

* James Heaton, "The Difference between Branding and Marketing," *Tronviggroup .com*, accessed October 28, 2017, http://www.tronviggroup.com/the-difference -between-marketing-and-branding/.

The goal of a branding game may not be to market something. As Heaton says above, "[Branding] is communication of characteristics, values, and attributes that clarify what this particular brand is and is not." Branding is more about building loyalty and maintaining customers who become fans and evangelists of the product or service, who then bring in more customers.* A brand wants passionate fans in its corner. (Need we discuss the avid customers in Mac vs. PC or iPhone vs. Samsung debates?) Chipotle released a mobile app, *Chipotle Scarecrow*, as part of a campaign with the same name. The aim of both the game and campaign is to raise awareness about food sustainability and Chipotle's commitment to avoid processed foods.† It wants to drive the conversation about the way food should and shouldn't be produced, and it wants people who will buy into and support its message.

A branding game has a specific *target audience*. Brands use games to reach that audience. We often design games with the game genre in mind, which comes with a built-in audience that has expectations for that genre. However, the brand's target audience needs to inform the game's design. Who that audience is should influence everything about the game, including its narrative design.‡

---

old spice: youland (2016): play the commercials! now live the commercials! now play...

Old Spice's Repositioning

Starting in 2010, Old Spice (Proctor & Gamble), with advertising agency Wieden+Kennedy, has created an iconic series of commercials that have gone viral on social media. The social media and TV advertisements take place in a world that's surreal with a bizarre sense of humor. They move from one high-impact, unexpected visual to the next.

---

* James Heaton, "The Difference between Branding and Marketing," Tronviggroup. com, accessed October 28, 2017, http://www.tronviggroup.com/the-difference -between-marketing-and-branding/.

† David Vinjamuri, "Chipotle Scarecrow Makes Enemies to Win Customers," *Forbes .com*, last modified September 13, 2013, https://www.forbes.com/sites/davidvinjamuri /2013/09/13/chipotle-scarecrow-makes-enemies-to-win-customers/#2d6068d2435a.

‡ Branding strategist Rachel Ginsberg, who leads strategy and partnerships for the Columbia University School of the Arts's Digital Storytelling Lab, also notes that "the brand's audience could potentially be targeted with a specific choice of [story] genre—hence a game writer's skill here is really valuable to a brand." Comment to author, January 16, 2018.

The commercials are a part of Old Spice's rebranding campaign. Old Spice was losing market shares to newer brand Axe and realized it had to reach a younger demographic. Axe, targeting young men, promoted itself as making men attractive to women.* In 2008, Old Spice released news ads with creative direction from agencies Wieden+Kennedy, Citizen Relations, and Landor.† The brand realized that women were the primary buyers of body wash, and they were buying women's body wash for their male partners.‡ Therefore, Old Spice needed to reach men *and* women. In 2010, Old Spice launched the "The Man Your Man Could Smell Like" ad campaign on YouTube. In the ad, Old Spice Guy addresses women and tells them to compare their man to him.§ With Old Spice, their man can be just like him.

The series "The Man Your Man Could Smell Like" features "Old Spice Guy," former NFL player Isaiah Mustafa. Some commercials feature him bare-chested and riding horseback on the beach, carrying a bouquet of roses, and sporting hyper-masculine, sexy poses. In other words, Mustafa's Old Spice Guy parodies romance novel tropes in order to appeal to both men and women.

---

* Megan O'Neill, "How Old Spice Swaggerized Their Brand and Men Everywhere," *Adweek.com*, last modified July 22, 2010, http://www.adweek.com/digital/how-old-spice-swaggerized-their-brand-and-men-everywhere/.

† "Old Spice: Manliness Redefined," *Landor.com*, last accessed October 28, 2017. https://landor.com/work/old-spice.

‡ "Case Study: Old Spice Response Campaign," *Dandad.org*, accessed October 28, 2017. https://www.dandad.org/en/d-ad-old-spice-case-study-insights/.

§ Sarah Rowe, "Old Spice Case Study," *ZonesofSMM.wordpress.com*, accessed October 28, 2017. https://zonesofsmm.wordpress.com/old-spice-case-study/.

"I'm on a horse"—one of Old Spice Guy's signature moments. Screenshot from Old Spice commercial produced by Wieden+Kennedy and is protected by United States and international copyright law. © Procter & Gamble

The ads' success led to more commercials in this surreal universe. In effect, Old Spice developed its own worldbuilding to contribute to its brand narrative.* Later in 2010, actor and former NFL player Terry Crews appeared in a series of Old Spice ads alone, and in 2015, with Isaiah Mustafa where they engaged in playful sparring, Mustafa as suave as ever, and Crews as Old Spice's id. Newer Old Spice ads feature every-mom, who sings her lamentation that she's losing her little boy as she spies on her son and his date. It's all Old Spice's fault for turning him into a man. Moms of several ethnicities spy on their sons as they slide down checkout counters, drag behind cars in laundry baskets as they hold onto the bumper, and trail behind the unsuspecting pair as their heads pop up from the sand on the beach and follow like land sharks.

* Ginsberg, comment to author, January 16, 2018.

"Dad Song," the response to "Mom Song," features the slogan "Gift a Boy into a Man." Screenshot from Old Spice commercial produced by Wieden+Kennedy and is protected by United States and international copyright law. © Procter & Gamble

Youland: 8-Bit Absurdity

Youland's title screen. Screenshot from *Old Spice: Youland*. Developed/produced by Wieden+Kennedy/MediaMonks and is protected by United States and international copyright law. © Procter & Gamble

Old Spice extended elements of its wacky advertising universe into *Old Spice: Youland*, developed by Wieden+Kennedy and MediaMonks. Launched on Facebook in 2016, the game places players in outlandish scenarios that could conceivably happen in Old Spice commercials. Additionally, it took data from players' Facebook accounts and used it in the game. The game plays up the "you" in *Youland* and personalizes the experience by constantly reminding players the game is all about "you."

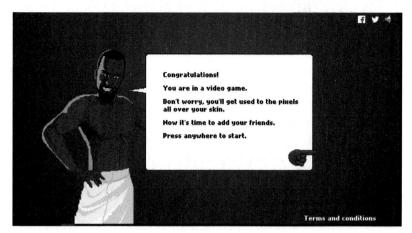

A familiar face serves as a guide character. Screenshot from *Old Spice: Youland*. Developed/ produced by Wieden+Kennedy/MediaMonks and is protected by United States and international copyright law. © Procter & Gamble

The player character's design used a personal photo of the player, warping it across the PC's face to make the PC look bizarre. While the game used photos from the players' Facebook profile, they could still customize the PC's hair and skin tone.

I'm hawt. Screenshot from *Old Spice: Youland*. Developed/produced by Wieden+Kennedy/MediaMonks and is protected by United States and international copyright law. © Procter & Gamble

The game also used data such as the player's age, liked pages, and snippets of posts to reference them in cutscenes. If players granted the game permission, they would see their friends appear as helpful or enemy NPCs.* Finally, creating the universe in pixel form would not be complete without Terry Crews and Isaiah Mustafa, who also lent their voices.

There are three mini games, each one corresponding to one of Old Spice's deodorant scents. Although the games' scenarios aren't based on the scents, cutscenes-as-advertisements pop up for the deodorant scent to spoof product placement.

Every part of the game's narrative design is straight out of Old Spice's fantastical, absurd world, taking into account the personalities and aesthetic that make its branding popular. On the loading screen, Terry Crews rides a tiger propelled by a flamethrower shooting out of its mouth. A fail screen features Crews and Mustafa, along with some animals and men dressed as food, at the player's funeral. In the opening cinematic for *Motorface*, a racing game that brings to mind Sega's *Crazy Taxi* and *Out Run*, Terry Crews greets the player as the player's Facebook friend is kidnapped along a desert highway. Crews is completely in character as he literally breaks the fourth wall by crashing through the desert background art and exposing a motherboard behind it. He tells players, "They made a videogame about you" and "You pixellate nice," as he shows the player a normal, undistorted photo. As the sports car snatches the friend and races away, he calls players "dummy" and yells at them to save their friend.

Screenshot from *Old Spice: Youland*. Developed/produced by Wieden+Kennedy/MediaMonks and is protected by United States and international copyright law. © Procter & Gamble

---

* "*Old Spice: Youland*," *Dutch Game Awards 2016*, accessed October 29, 2017, http://dutchgameawards.nl/2016/old-spice-youland/.

Screenshot from *Old Spice: Youland*. Developed/produced by Wieden+Kennedy/MediaMonks and is protected by United States and international copyright law. © Procter & Gamble

The Old Spice universe also heavily influences *Youland's* gameplay. In *Motorface*, player characters turn into cars as they power up. The art and animations provide the wacky visuals to match, as the PC acquires tires for hands, then a full front axle, and tiny feet in the back. Once the player is a full-fledged car, driving into Facebook friends collects them, and they agree to fuse themselves to the car, which makes it go faster. The game revels in the fact that it's ludicrous, telling players "Confusing but cool."

The player transforms into a car. Screenshot from *Old Spice: Youland*. Developed/produced by Wieden+Kennedy/MediaMonks and is protected by United States and international copyright law. © Procter & Gamble

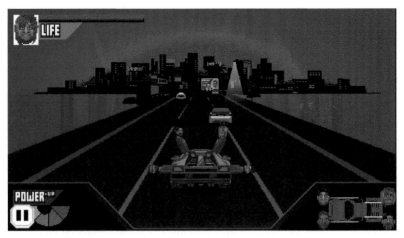

Facebook friends make up the car's spoilers and wings. Screenshot from *Old Spice: Youland*. Developed/produced by Wieden+Kennedy/MediaMonks and is protected by United States and international copyright law. © Procter & Gamble

Reaching Old Spice's Demographic

The mini game's story scenario plays up the interests of Old Spice's target demographic/audience. In *Fistful of Cash*, players are low-level employees who make their way out of the basement at their corporation to make it to the top of the executive ladder. Levels are floors of the building with enemies and a boss to beat. Health items and weapons improve from floor to floor, including discarded boxes of Chinese takeout; stacks of cash and gold bars for health; and tape dispensers, swordfish, and cacti for ammo.

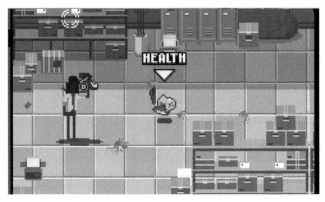

Screenshot from *Old Spice: Youland*. Developed/produced by Wieden+Kennedy/MediaMonks and is protected by United States and international copyright law. © Procter & Gamble

Once players climb "all of the ladders of life" and become wealthy, they have to deal with fake friends, celebrities, and sycophants—like something out of an unhinged reality show. (Okay, so a lot of reality shows are unhinged, but you know what I mean.) *Fistful of Cash* takes the feelings that a lot of young people have about their lives, wanting a better job that affords a better lifestyle. As always, though, the game doesn't condescend to players. It laughs with them.

Screenshot from *Old Spice: Youland.* Developed/produced by Wieden+Kennedy/MediaMonks and is protected by United States and international copyright law. © Procter & Gamble

While it's a safe bet to say that many of Old Spice's loyal customers and fans play videogames, putting out a game with such bizarre gameplay and art could attract other gamers to play. In this way, *Old Spice: Youland* serves as both a gift to those who already follow the brand and an effective marketing tool to reach new potential customers.

planning the branding game's narrative design

What do you do if you're a narrative designer or writer who finds yourself on a development team for a branding game, and you've had little or no experience in advertising? I worked on two branding games. Each time, I was hired as the narrative designer to join the development team. In both instances, the games were never released, and I can't go into detail about them (nondisclosure agreements are fun). However, I can share what I learned from both of those projects.

I mentioned earlier that you'll need to change your perspective a little. Typically, we don't think of a target audience/demographic as a focal point when designing games. We might consider player expectations and types of players and what they enjoy/what frustrates them when it comes to the game's genre or story. The driving force of the design is not *who* the player is. However, the brand has a goal, and the brand is trying to reach a very specific target audience. So, the goal and the target audience need to be at the heart of the project's game design and narrative design.

It's *extremely* important that the champion of the story (whether that person is called "narrative designer" or "game writer"*) be a part of the initial planning and be in meetings or on calls with those representing the brand. Simply hearing or reading what the brand wants is no substitute for hearing it for oneself and being able to ask follow-up questions and have follow-up discussions. As a part of the initial planning, the champion of the story contributes to brainstorming and can give immediate feedback to ideas the brand may have. If an idea doesn't quite work, the narrative designer or the writer can offer suggestions *before* further work is put in that will have to be discarded, wasting time and money. The narrative designer or game writer can also help the brand and developer flesh out preliminary ideas and concepts and the project's scope.

initial consultation phase

During your initial contacts with the brand, you want to get a clear understanding of the brand and the project. Brands have personalities. They have specific ways of communicating, and followers of the brand (and target demographic) will expect it to communicate in certain ways. For example, since 2008, Old Spice's ads have been wacky, surreal, and playfully nonsensical at times. If their tone suddenly changed, the atmosphere became that of a serious political thriller, and Old Spice Guy became a scruffy secret service agent sitting in a

---

* Narrative designers get called game writers and vice versa, although the two roles are different. Also, you may find yourself taking on a bit of both roles on any one project.

posh nightclub, that would be a needle scratch for everyone familiar with the brand.

You want to review all documentation the brand provides to the development team. That sounds obvious, but if you're a subcontractor and not an employee, you sometimes have to make these requests. Get access to everything the brand explains about itself, its target audience, and the game it wants to make: information that documents the brand's strategy and persona (the human-like qualities it attributes to itself), and get a detailed, clear brief, as well as the target audience's demographic and psychographic information.* (For more on demographics and psychographics, see "Reaching the Target Audience" later in this chapter.)

understanding the brand

The brand may or may not have made a game before. I've worked with several clients who were totally new to game development, including the two who wanted branding games. Questions I like to ask are: Why now? Why is this the right time to make a game? Why is a game the right way to reach your target audience? These types of questions can give you insight about the brand's goals and how it intends to reach its target audience.

Also, it's important to know if the brand has tried to reach this target audience through campaigns before. Were those campaigns successful? What did and didn't work?

Get to Know the Brand's Story

Brand stories aren't traditional narratives with plots and characters. They embody the values of the brand. Chipotle's brand story is that it believes in food sustainability, supporting farmers, and avoiding GMO ingredients. Furthermore, it desires to provide its customers with high-quality, healthier food options with the speed of fast-food restaurants. This isn't something Chipotle has to constantly advertise through slogans. Consumers know all of this because they've learned this to be true about Chipotle—a critical component of the brand story. Case in point: Chipotle's slogan is "Food with Integrity." *E. coli* outbreaks at its restaurants in 2015 greatly challenged the

---

* Ginsberg, comment to author, January 16, 2018.

brand and turned away loyal customers. However, Chipotle openly addressed the safety issues and apologized in targeted campaigns around the affected restaurants. This transparency illustrated the brand's integrity and story, which brought customers back to these restaurants.*

Brand stories inspire emotional reactions and connections (again, Mac vs. PC, anyone?). Products and services, vision, purpose, design, community, location, and reputation are some of the things that create a brand story's makeup.†

The development team must incorporate the brand's story into the game. The brand story must be the essence that informs everything from the game's mechanics to its art and sound. Unlike print, TV, or online advertising and marketing, a game allows players to engage with the brand story, reinforcing it and making it more relatable. For example, in *Chipotle Scarecrow*, players save animals from harsh factory environments, plant crops, and provide people with wholesome food alternatives instead of the prepackaged meals they're used to eating. They act out Chipotle's goals through gameplay.

researching the target audience

Research is an absolute must in any storyteller's toolkit, as Megan Fausti discusses in Chapter 7. Research helps us use real-world inspirations in our worldbuilding, analyze historical figures to design our characters' psychologies, and reverse engineer plot arcs to come up with the ebb and flow of our own story campaigns' conflicts. Put those same researching skills to work for branding games, but what you first research may be a little different than what you're used to.

The Target Audience's Demographics and Psychographics

The brand has a definite target demographic. You can think of these individuals as an audience. If you've worked on stories for other media, you know the value of understanding the target audience. This audience has specific expectations. They're attracted to certain types of

---

* Sophie Bakalar, "What Chipotle Can Teach Companies about Honesty with Customers," *Fortune*, last updated June 24, 2017, http://fortune.com/2017/06/24 /transparency-chipotle-customer-loyalty/.

† Bernadette Jiwa, "20 Keys to a Brand Story," *The Story of Telling*, last accessed October 29, 2017, http://thestoryoftelling.com/what-is-a-brand-story/.

plots and characters, and they assume the stories they enjoy will have certain genre conventions. You can think of the target audience of your game in a similar fashion, although now you'll want to apply who they are to what they may or may not enjoy about the brand.

While demographics are a familiar concept, psychographics may not be, especially if you haven't been around marketing perspectives. Demographics focus on who people are. Their age, race, ethnicity, sexual orientation, religion, marital status, household income, number of children, level of education (among other things)—you can use any of these to categorize people into specific groups. Demographics deal in generalities.

Psychographics add a shade of complexity that demographics do not. Psychographics get at the heart of why people believe what they do and behave the way they do. They can be as detailed as explaining why people have certain hobbies. They help us understand people's values. Because demographics generalize, they don't establish how the people in the same group can be different. Psychographics, however, pinpoint the nuances of their lifestyles by "[measuring] customers' attitudes and interests."* In order to effectively reach the target audience, we need to understand both their demographics and psychographics. This, of course, requires research, and representatives of the brand—unless the brand is new—should be able to provide you this information. Understanding the target audience's demographics and psychographics will help you better plan the types of stories and scenarios that would appeal to them. Specifically, you can use the audience's likes, dislikes, needs, and wants to influence the mechanics' narrative design, story genre, plot scenarios, and characters.

Research Topics

Most clients I've worked with already had an idea for their game's story. How much of a developed idea varied. Some had a one-line scenario. Others had major characters and conflicts planned out, while one client had certain philosophical ideas to espouse, but no idea for the story. Whether the development team is responsible for coming up with the game's story or not, the client will have the ultimate say

---

* Alexandra Samuel, "Psychographics Are Just as Important for Marketers as Demographics," *Harvard Business Review*, last updated March 11, 2016, https://hbr.org/2016/03/psychographics-are-just-as-important-for-marketers-as-demographics.

in what it is and how that story evolves or changes throughout production. Most likely, the individuals representing the brand won't be writers themselves. But, whether they're set on a particular concept or not, you can help them understand what their target audience likes about the stories it consumes. Therefore, some of your research can help fine-tune the story and gameplay concepts and explain why these are best suited for the target audience.

I found researching the types of stories the target audience consumes extremely helpful. For example, we can generalize and say, "Women readers love urban fantasy." Okay. Why? What about its genre conventions appeals to them? Are some subgenres of urban fantasy more popular with women over others? How about more specific demographics? What subgenres are women ages 35–40 reading? Your demographics and psychographics can narrow down and focus your research.

For one of the branding games I worked on, I already had a pretty good idea of the types of stories the target audience consumed. In my initial search, I looked up what the target audience (young adults) watched and read when it came to films, TV shows, books, and comics/manga. I looked at what was on novel and comics/manga bestseller lists and the top-grossing films for that demographic over the past two years. As is often the case, what I discovered led to more avenues of research. For example, "Sick lit" was popular. So, I started comparing and contrasting films and books with protagonists who were dealing with illness.

When I reported back to the development team and the client, I had a doc that explained what the target demographic was reading and watching, breaking down the similarities in stories, characters, and themes. We applied these to all of our potential story scenarios.

Give the client a few options to choose from. As you talk with the brand representatives, be prepared to reword and revise these ideas. The options may not be what the brand is looking for, or they may require some tweaking, such as refining content for the target audience, whether that content is the plot, characters, overall message/philosophy the brand wants to include, etc. Additionally, you may have to rework some of your ideas if they cause the project to be outside of the brand's budget or they're limited by technology.

finalizing the plan

Once you finish your initial phase and research, work closely with the rest of the development team to come up with narrative design and story delivery that will be in concert with the game design. As we've been echoing throughout this book, *everybody* on the team needs to be involved in the process. Every game needs programmers, artists, sound designers, composers, animators, game designers, and level designers contributing to its narrative design.

After you get the go-ahead from the brand to proceed with your plan, the level of communication you have with its representatives will vary. I spoke to one client by phone every week. Another client didn't communicate with the development team until we approached a milestone.

conclusion

As is so often the case in game development, plans change, so be flexible. Assets get removed. Levels get replaced, etc. Anything can happen for any number of reasons, from clients having to cut back on scope because funding slowed to clients simply changing their minds, for any number of reasons.

when working on branding games...

Understand the brand and its story. A brand is about more than selling something. Brands have specific values and philosophies to attract consumers and turn them into loyal fans and evangelists.

Know the brand's target audience's demographics and psychographics. The branding game will have a specific target audience the brand wants to reach. Knowing who members of the target audience are and what they're interested in will help you formulate a plan for the game's narrative design.

What are the game's social elements? Brands have used social games as a way to reach new customers. Often, inviting friends, sending them resources daily, asking them for resources in return, and posting in-game exploits to feeds

have been the social components. Are there other ways players can interact in-game or on social media?

Use research to fine-tune the game's narrative design. Your target
audience consumes certain types of film, TV, comics/manga,
and prose fiction. What they like can help inform both gameplay and story.

branding checklist

- Have you asked the brand representatives questions that will
help you understand their goals for the project and their target audience?
- Is your plan for the game's narrative design in agreement with
the brand's story?
- Does your plan for the game's narrative design fit within the
brand's budget and the project's scope?
- Are there elements of the narrative design that *may not* appeal
to the target audience?

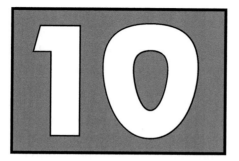

the continued adventures
writing for licensed mobile games

Jessica Sliwinski

contents

introduction

As any fan of a hit television show knows, the weeks between new episodes can be torture. Fans of blockbuster films or book series have it even worse, waiting years or more for sequels or new installments. Many fans pass the time by creating their own works set in that universe, but for those without the time, talent, or inclination to do so, licensed videogames can help bridge the gap, providing immersive experiences within a beloved universe on the player's terms and time-table. The history of licensed games is a bumpy one; at one time synonymous with rushed, buggy, and critical and commercial failures, the genre has seen a renaissance of late as more and more properties are expanded into franchises, allowing them to retain public interest over an indefinite period of time. With a more luxurious development schedule no longer chained to the inexorable approach of a single TV show, film, or book series's release date, we have seen the rise of licensed games that not only rival their source material, but also often surpass it. Console games such as Telltale's *The Walking Dead*, Ubisoft's *South Park: The Stick of Truth* and *South Park: The Fractured but Whole*, and Rocksteady's *Batman: Arkham* series have all been lauded for their faithfulness to their source material, as well as demonstrating a clear understanding of what fans find appealing about their respective licenses. As AAA hits go, so goes the industry, and licenses are also being embraced by mobile game companies, seeking (among other boons) instant brand recognition in a glutted market.

But too often, licenses are used and abused as either 1) slick packaging for a shoddy product or 2) unrecognizable packaging that not only scares players off from a potentially great game but also damages the license itself. These sins have been and continue to be committed in game development for all platforms, but are especially egregious when committed on mobile, a platform that already faces accusations of being nonsubstantive fluff, designed only to prey on addictive tendencies in pursuit of a quick buck. When it comes to licensed games, the mobile platform actually offers unique benefits to both the licensor and the licensee that other platforms cannot. For the licensor, perhaps the greatest of these is the opportunity to greatly expand their audience: far more people own mobile devices and play mobile games than consoles or PCs. While console and PC gaming is becoming more and more cloud-based and social, mobile remains the ultimate social platform: if a licensor wants to see fans connecting and evangelizing about their favorite TV show, film, or book series, there are few better or easier places to do so than within a mobile game, especially one with multiplayer features that allow players to feel like they are part of a real community of like-minded fans.

For the licensee, the aforementioned brand recognition is a time and money saver in more ways than at the point of purchase:

utilizing a preexisting license allows developers to spend less time on worldbuilding and brand establishment, and more time on making a great game. But securing a license for a game should not be viewed as the means to an end; rather, the license *is* the end. When making a licensed mobile game, developers should strive to create an experience that is as thrilling as any of the critical console successes listed above, as well as an authentic reminder of the player's original encounter with the license. If the developers are not fans of the license at the start of development, by the end they should understand and appreciate why that license has so many fans, if they have not become fans themselves. For the writer, this becomes especially important, as the text is both technically the easiest place to show off a developer's profound understanding of the license, as well as the most obvious example of a profound *mis*understanding. This chapter will outline how to treat a license with the same respect and care as any fan as well as how to address the unique challenges of creating immersive experiences within that license on a mobile platform.

general theory and best practices: writing for licenses

The first step for a writer of a licensed game on any platform is to establish a relationship with the licensor. There are often preexisting prejudices on both sides: the licensor fears the writer will damage the license they have so painstakingly established and fought to protect over the years, while the writer fears the licensor exists only to say "no" to everything. But in actuality, the attentive licensor should be appreciated and even embraced. It is the cavalier licensor who should be feared, as they may not possess a clear understanding or appreciation of the license they have been tasked with protecting. The attentive licensor who pays attention and offers detailed notes is as concerned with getting it right as the writer of a licensed game is (or should be). The licensor is not the writer's enemy, but their partner, and is there to help ensure that the final product enhances the license rather than damages it.

Help, My Licensor Is a Jerk!

It's often a challenge to find a common vision between a licensor and a licensee. But sometimes, not everyone working at a licensing office has a common vision of a license, or are even fans of it. Licenses owned by vast corporations are often managed by an equally vast department within that corporation that oversees licensing for many different products besides videogames. Licenses with upcoming, unreleased content that are prone to frequent hacks or leaks may be unwilling or unable to provide guidance on this content to even the most trusted licensee. Under these circumstances, a licensor's feedback may be scattershot, vague, contradictory, confusing, inaccurate, or missing entirely. What's the writer of a licensed game to do?

First, remember that licensors are humans too, and even they can forget or confuse the minutiae of a particularly large license; this is not necessarily a sign of incompetence or neglect. Secondly, remember that licensors are rarely ever editors or writers themselves. The feedback they provide may be as unfiltered as it might be coming from a player, and it is important for a writer to be able to look beyond their immediate umbrage and discover the root of the problem. When feedback seems incomplete or otherwise unhelpful, remain professional and seek collaboration, or consider new ways of approaching the licensor in order to get the information you need.

While many of the macro questions—genre/platform of game, major game systems, the overall premise within the larger universe of the license—will likely have been answered already as part of the pitch process for securing the license, there are still several important questions a writer should ask/answer during early interactions with the licensor. These include the following:

- *What are the core elements of this license?* George Lucas's *Star Wars* revolves around a broken family struggling with the duality of light and darkness within all men, played out in the context of an epic galactic war featuring spaceships, aliens, and wizards with magical powers and glowing swords of light. Adam Reed's *Archer* asks what would happen when a group of selfish, immature, stunted adolescents in adult bodies are tasked with the complicated, highly dangerous work of international espionage. Stephen King's *The Dark Tower* invites readers into a world where time and space are fluid, and only one ancient mystery matters: what is the Dark Tower, will the gunslinger reach it, and will the sacrifices he makes along the way be worth the journey? Whether film, television, book, or other origin, all licenses have core elements that identify them as such. These elements are and should be present in all good iterations of that license, and can very often be found lacking in bad ones. The *Star Wars* prequels (*Episodes I–III*), for example, are often dinged for focusing less on family dynamics and more on the complex politics of a fictional body of government, which were not a core element of the original *Star Wars* trilogy. The newest *Star Wars* films (*Episode VII* and counting), however, have been lauded for a return to form: here is the broken family, struggling with the duality of light and darkness within all men, played out in the context of an epic galactic war featuring spaceships, aliens, and wizards with magical powers and glowing swords of light.

- *What has/hasn't worked best for this license?* Among *Star Trek* fans, the series *Deep Space Nine* can be a polarizing one. For all the fans who appreciate its darker themes and moral ambiguity, there are just as many who deride these elements as untrue to the franchise as a whole. For these detractors, morality in *Star Trek* is clear, and Starfleet officers should always be on the side of the angels. If it is not entirely accurate to call *Deep Space Nine* the "black sheep" of the *Star Trek* license, it is at least accurate to say that it stands out from its sister series as a horse of a different color. A licensor may be wary of things that haven't worked as well as desired in the past and be more eager to stick with a tried and true formula—or the licensor may feel it's time to shake things up and experiment within the bounds of the license! It is important to fully understand any "baggage" that comes with a license, whether it is the safety of its successes or the scars of its failures.

- *Are there any specific restrictions or sacred cows within this license?* Similar to core elements but on a smaller scale, the sacred cows of a license are its beloved characters, concepts, or other items, which, if perceived to have been negatively tampered with, could result in revolt or protest from not only the license's fans, but also its creators. During development of the MMORPG *Star Wars: The Old Republic*, Yoda and Yoda's yet unnamed species were considered sacred cows of the *Star Wars* license. Creating a new character of the same species as Yoda or attempting to establish new facts regarding this species was only permitted after a vigorous vetting process from the licensor, to ensure that Yoda's own legacy and reputation would not be tarnished by lesser successors.

- *Will this game be considered canon?* Whether or not a licensed game is considered *canon*—i.e., the events of that game are considered to be permanent, real events within the timeline of the license, and must be referred to or otherwise considered throughout the license in perpetuity—can have far more impact than many licensors or developers realize. If a licensed game is considered canon, creating content for that game comes with far more restrictions. The writer must leave as many doors open for future licensed content as possible; taking drastic actions, such as killing off a beloved character or changing the nature of the world the characters live in, may not be permitted. Introducing new characters, creatures, technology, or other concepts is also viewed with much more scrutiny, as these will become permanent parts of the license. If a licensed game is *not* considered canon, the writer may be allowed far more latitude in creating content, since as far as the licensor is concerned, the events of the game take place in an alternate reality that can be discarded or disavowed as desired in future licensed products. This is often to the project's benefit, as not having to fit within a specific series of canonical events allows game writers to tell a more powerful story. The owners of the Marvel copyright, for instance, recently made it clear that they would not require Marvel licensed games to adhere to the ever-expanding Marvel universe. "We want to give [developers] freedom to tell their story, and we want to make it an original story," said Marvel Games Creative Director Bill Roseman to IGN at DICE 2017.*

- *What FCC/MPAA rating has this license earned? What ESRB rating (hypothetical or otherwise) is desired for the game?* In order to consider the audience for a licensed game, the writer must first consider the audience for the license. What is the demographic (particularly the age group) the license targets? What are the content standards for that license's typical platform, and does the license abide by them, push the limits,

---

* Jonathon Dornbush, "Marvel Games to Tell Original Stories, Not Held to Canon," *IGN.com*, last modified February 23, 2017, http://www.ign.com/articles/2017/02/24 /dice-2017-marvel-games-to-tell-original-stories-not-held-to-canon.

or self-restrict themselves even further in order to be true to the license? Oftentimes, a writer will find that a license's typical platform presents different challenges and opportunities than videogame platforms. HBO broadcasts *Game of Thrones*, for example, on a premium subscriber-based network, allowing great latitude in portraying violence and sexuality. The ESRB, however, has strict content standards for rating games, preventing any game based on *Game of Thrones* from matching the more prurient experience of watching the show without earning an Adults Only (AO) rating. But these aspects are core elements of the dark, brutal fantasy epic that is *Game of Thrones*. It is thus up to the writer of a licensed *Game of Thrones* game to find a way to remain true to the license while abiding by the platform's content standards. Disruptor Beam's *Game of Thrones Ascent* solved this problem by imagining how the HBO series would be depicted on network or basic cable instead of a premium channel, and creating content to suit. The game never visually depicts graphic sexual content or violence and alludes to it, rather than describing it in detail in the text. We will examine *Game of Thrones Ascent* more closely in Case Study #1 later in this chapter.

- *How far and in what directions can the existing canon of the license be expanded?* Is the writer permitted to introduce new characters, settings, events, items, laws of physics, or other elements to the existing universe, or is the writer limited to the universe as established by the license holder? Can the writer retcon or expand upon the existing history of the license, or is that history set in stone? Can the writer move the characters beyond where they were last seen in the source material, or is the writer limited to writing what amounts to prequels or concurrent adventures? Often, these restrictions are informed as much by other licensed products in development as the licensor's personal preferences. A good licensor ensures that all its products are complementary and have a symbiotic relationship, each expanding and enhancing the license in their own way, rather than competing with each other.

- *What are the expectations in regards to an approvals process or a content creation pipeline?* The most attentive licensors will play every new build of a licensed game in development, offering critique not only on the written words but also on gameplay, user experience design, artwork, and more. Less attentive licensors will wash their hands of the business immediately after a license is secured, allowing a game company to do whatever they like with it. Most licensors fall somewhere in between; they may restrict themselves to only reviewing text and artwork with occasional playthroughs of the game itself, and/or establish a set of guidelines and example content up front that are assumed to be followed throughout development. Sometimes, the licensor must approve content before it can be implemented into even an internal build, and sometimes a licensor will allow unapproved content to go live if the licensor has not been able to review it in a timely manner. Whatever the licensor's preferences, it is important to identify them up front and abide by them throughout development, lest the licensor discover objectionable content shortly before ship. In a best-case scenario, this could force hurried rewrites; in a worst-case scenario, the licensor could deny permission to ship a game entirely!

All of these questions are designed to address the same overarching concern: *what is the licensor's understanding of this license, and does it match the writer's?* If not, both parties must make adjustments until they agree on what the license is and why it is so special to so many people. Only then is the writer in a position to create an authentic licensed game.

As established above, a good relationship with a licensor is essential. But that said, a licensor is a partner, not an editor. The buck stops with the writer; no one will look more foolish if a licensed game is accused of being poorly or inauthentically written. The most important thing any writer of a licensed videogame can do to ensure quality is to know the license inside and out. Watch, read, play, and otherwise consume all works that comprise the license. Read critical commentary on the license. Visit websites and forums where fans discuss their love of (and their gripes with) the license. The better a writer's understanding of a license, the better equipped he or she is to create new material within the confines of that license, with minimal revisions as requested by the licensor. Deep knowledge of a license can also help improve the relationship with the licensor, who is often told how well the writer knows the license, but doesn't really know for sure until it is demonstrated through the writer's work. The most important result of this process, however, is that the writer comes away with a clear understanding of why this license is beloved by its fans and continues to endure over countless others jostling for the public's attention. It is not a requirement that the writers themselves be a fan of the license (although it certainly helps!), but they must at least understand why so many others are.

general theory and best practices: licensed mobile games

Like many aspects of writing for mobile games, guidelines for writing licensed content come down to questions of timing. Unlike their console or PC counterparts, mobile games are designed to be played in short stints, multiple times a day. The explosion of the mobile gaming industry means that at any given time, a mobile game is competing not just with physical boxes on a brick-and-mortar store shelf, but also with literally millions of other titles on virtual shelves with no maximum capacity. Lastly, most mobile games are free to download, if not strictly free to play, meaning that if a player decides he has made an error in acquiring the game, he can easily remove it from his device and move on to a competing product at no personal cost. Securing a well-known and beloved license is no longer a surefire path to a popular and/or profitable launch; licensors rarely offer exclusivity, and players can afford to be picky. Writers of licensed mobile games should therefore adhere to the following guidelines if they want their games to be successful:

- *Establish the license immediately.* A good rule of thumb for writing in any medium is to grab the reader's attention at once. When writing for a licensed mobile game, this rule can be refined to establish the license at once. The player needs to know within the first few seconds of play that this is a *Star Trek* game, or a *Futurama* game, or a *Final Fantasy* game. While a game's graphics and other visuals aid greatly in communicating this, narrative design and writing also play a large role. For example, in *Kim Kardashian: Hollywood*, the first thing the player sees upon starting the game is a video of Kim Kardashian herself in the flesh, welcoming them to the game. The player's first in-game quest immediately following involves assisting an animated, in-game version of Kim Kardashian with a fashion emergency. The player knows immediately that this is a game built around the

Kim Kardashian license, where she can expect to encounter the Kardashian family on a regular basis and live out the fantasy of becoming a celebrity in Hollywood.

- *Immerse the player in the world of the license.* On the other side of the coin, developers should not place the full burden of establishing the license on the main narrative delivery systems within a mobile game. The player can and should be immersed in the license outside the context of story, in aspects of the game that often fall under the purview of the writer, but are just as often their lowest priority. UX text such as button labels, error or more-info pop-ups, tutorial instructions, item descriptions, and more should not be considered chores, but rather additional opportunities to enrich a licensed product. In EA's *The Simpsons: Tapped Out*, the player gains experience points and levels up at regular intervals, a ubiquitous mechanic seen in many games. While it would suffice for the text in the "Level Up" pop-up to simply read, "Congratulations, you have leveled up!," the writers of *The Simpsons: Tapped Out* instead chose to imbue this moment with licensed flavor. Upon the player's first "Level Up" moment, which occurs during the game tutorial, Bart Simpson appears next to the sarcastic text, "Wow, you put the house down where it told you to." An otherwise routine, pedestrian moment is suddenly transformed into a laugh worthy of the license, all from a single string of text.

- *Choose the right narrative design for the license AND the platform.* Though the genre of mobile game—roleplaying, creature collection, war, massively multiplayer, etc.—may be set in stone long before the writer is brought in, he or she still has the opportunity to ensure the narrative design is the best fit for the license. Consider the tone and pacing of the license itself. Is it frenetic, with huge action set pieces interspersed with quiet character moments, a la *The Fast and the Furious*? A linear storyline that does not require or allow player choice might be best. Is it quiet and frequently introspective, a la *The Dark Tower*? A roleplaying game with multiple side quests that allow full exploration of this mysterious world would likely fit the bill. Whatever the tone and pacing of the license, it should be mirrored in the tone and pacing of a licensed mobile game.

However, it is also imperative to keep the mobile platform in mind when considering the narrative design of a licensed game. As established throughout this book, the habits of the mobile gamer differ greatly from those of console or PC gamers. Mobile game players rarely engage with a game for long stints, preferring multiple short play sessions of no longer than 15 minutes over the course of a day. Each of these sessions must feel equally satisfying to players, leaving them with both a sense of accomplishment and the need to keep going. Licenses that feature long or complicated storylines that are revealed slowly over time can be a challenge to evoke on a mobile platform, which often seems best suited to single-serving storylines that do not require the player to retain knowledge between play sessions. In these instances, the mobile game writer should seize upon the aspects of the license that are best suited to the mobile platform. In Kabam's *Marvel Contest of Champions*, the epic clashes between superheroes and villains that fill the pages of comic books form the spine of the game's narrative design. In each play session, the player faces a new or returning opponent, who is introduced, fought, and defeated within a single play session. This design is well suited to the habits of the mobile gamer while remaining true to the core elements of the license itself.

- *Target casual fans before superfans.* Far more people own a mobile device than own a console or PC, greatly expanding the potential audience for any mobile game. Therefore, writers of licensed mobile games would do well to cast their nets wide in appealing to fans of a license. Frequent and prominent references to esoteric trivia or other minutiae of an established license may score points with superfans, but are also likely to alienate more casual fans, who may begin to feel as though they are not big enough fans of the license to enjoy the game. If this occurs, it is a double blow to both the game developer and the licensor: licenses are granted in order to expand that license's audience, not narrow it. This is not to say that demonstrating deep knowledge of a license should be avoided entirely, but consider carefully the timing and placement of such demonstrations within a licensed game.

- *Strive to rival a console or PC licensed game experience.* Though the mobile game industry has developed its share of corporate titans, many mobile game developers often feel as though they are the independent little guy struggling to survive against big competitors with vast resources and enormous reach. When coupled with the very real limitations of time, money, and headcounts, this mentality can often lead to mobile game developers settling on the quality of their products, convinced that they could never hope to rival their console or PC counterparts. If this mentality is detrimental to the development of mobile games in general, it is an absolute death sentence for licensed mobile games, which already face a double stigma. Writers of licensed mobile games should thus approach the project with the same level of enthusiasm and care as they would an AAA console or PC project, which also see their fair share of complications due to insufficient time, money, or headcounts. There is no reason why a licensed mobile game can't have a rich and engaging story, or a cinematic trailer, or a conversation system in which the player gets a say in where the story goes. The platform may alter the size and scope of a feature, but it should never dissuade a writer from doing what is best for the game.

case studies: introduction

Each case study in this chapter examines a game that utilizes a license popular at the time of publication. This is not to say that only licenses that are vastly and/or currently popular are worth turning into a mobile game, but rather to explore how these games—which share virtual shelf space with several other games based off the same popular license—are able to capture the attention of players at a time when their respective licenses are at peak audience saturation.

All of the games featured in this chapter also utilize the "freemium" pricing strategy. A freemium game is one in which the player may download, install, and play the game for free, but may also choose to unlock premium features, additional functionality, and/or high-quality virtual goods via microtransaction. Again, this is not to say that only freemium licensed games are well executed, but an acknowledgement of the fact that freemium is the dominant (and, arguably, the most successful) model in the history of mobile game development thus far.

Lastly, as a matter of full disclosure, I served as a Lead Narrative Designer for all three case study games.

Case Study #1: *Game of Thrones Ascent* (2013)

Rival families, medieval history, destiny versus free will, and a gritty fantasy of fire and ice: these are the core elements that have drawn so many to HBO's *Game of Thrones* television series, based on the book series *A Song of Ice and Fire* by George R. R. Martin. Disruptor Beam's *Game of Thrones Ascent* seeks to expand this intriguing world by allowing the player themselves to join the game of thrones, fighting on behalf of their favorite great house while trying to advance their own vassal house's fortunes along the way.

The core elements of the *Game of Thrones* license are reinforced during the first play session, in which the player defeats slavers at the request of the king, is awarded a patent of nobility, begins constructing his Keep, selects his background (and thus, perhaps, his destiny), swears his oath of fealty to a great house, enters a brothel in search of answers, and sees his fair daughter lose a hand to a gangrenous wound. Immediately, the player realizes that, like *Game of Thrones* itself, this is a dark and gritty world where not even those closest to him are safe from personal tragedy.

The game's storyline is primarily delivered via quests that include an RPG-esque conversation system. This not only reinforces the inherent roleplay already present in the license, where each great house has a specific reputation and known strengths/weaknesses, but it also caters to both casual fans and superfans. Casual fans have the room and opportunity to ask questions about concepts they may not be familiar with, while superfans may bypass as desired further explanation of things they already know.

Game of Thrones Ascent's quest system is also structured with the platform in mind. In addition to the text-based quests described above, which take only as long to complete as is necessary to read and select a response, the game also features timed "Sworn Sword" quests, in which the player can dispatch one of several fighters, tradesmen, or spies at his command to perform actions necessary to advance the plot. Sworn Sword quests take time to complete, meaning that the player may quickly send out his swords in one short play session, then return later for another short play session to see how they fared, providing a compelling reengagement mechanic.

Game of Thrones Ascent also immerses the player in the license beyond the quest system. During mobile game tutorials, oftentimes a character will appear to explain various game systems one by one to the player, a common tactic that can instantly break immersion, especially if mobile games do not exist in that character's world. Rather than have a *Game of Thrones* character instruct the player where to tap, *Game of Thrones Ascent* has the characters provide narrative context for what the player is doing, then utilizes nondialogue-based instructional tooltips to direct the player's fingers.

This attention to detail persists beyond the tutorial, from framing partnerships with other players at a betrothal to reliving favorite plot points from *Game of Thrones* as tales being reenacted for the player's amusement.

Perhaps the most unique aspect of *Game of Thrones Ascent* is its commitment to providing content related to the ongoing television series in as close to real time as possible. From seasons 1 to 5, the writers were allowed access to the same early cuts of episodes as members of the press weeks before they aired. This allowed the team to create quest content related to that episode's events and release it the day after the episode aired, a concept they promoted as "Watch on Sunday, play on Monday!" Fans of *Game of Thrones* could watch an episode, spend the week actively becoming a part of it in *Game of Thrones Ascent*, then enjoy the next episode at the end of the week, eagerly anticipating how that episode would be integrated into the game the next morning.

Though increased security for seasons 6 and 7 of the HBO show prevented the *Game of Thrones Ascent* writers from viewing the episodes ahead of their air date, they remained committed to delivering related content as quickly as possible, writing, implementing, and releasing it within a week of each episode's air date instead. While the slimmed down technological demands of the mobile platform make this goal more achievable, the goal itself seeks to rival the experience of a licensed console or PC game, which might be more expected to have the ambition necessary to achieve it. From the prologue to "Volume VII" and counting, *Game of Thrones Ascent* offers an experience as rich, immersive, and thrilling as watching the HBO series itself—only in 15-minute increments instead of a full hour.

Case Study #2: *Star Trek Timelines* (2016)

Set in the distant future, *Star Trek* imagines a galaxy where humanity has overcome their racial, social, and cultural differences and united in the spirit of exploration and discovery. Once we begin encountering new life and civilizations on other worlds, however, our own codes of morality are called into question, and we are forced to answer, again and again, "What does it mean to be human?" Disruptor Beam's *Star Trek Timelines* creates an strange new world, in which a series of temporal anomalies defy the laws of time and space, bringing together people, places, and objects from the past, present, future, and alternate realities. The player is tasked with sorting out the chaos this has caused, as well as continuing to seek out both what spawned these anomalies and how they might be reversed.

Like *Game of Thrones Ascent*, *Star Trek Timelines* immediately establishes the license and pushes the boundaries of the mobile platform within the first few moments of the game. The game opens with a cinematic using real game assets, in which the player's ship and a Romulan escort encounter the first of many temporal anomalies the player will see throughout the course of the game. Shortly afterwards, the player encounters James T. Kirk, the original captain of the Enterprise, as well as Michael Burnham, the newest leading lady of the newest *Star Trek* series, *Discovery*. This decision captures not only casual fans and superfans, but also fans of the 1960s and the present day. By casting the audience net wide, *Star Trek Timelines* ensures every new player feels welcomed.

Captain James T. Kirk

"Jim Kirk. I don't know our friend here or why the Enterprise is out there without me, but there's no time—those Romulan vessels are preparing to fire. Give us orders, captain!"

TAP TO CONTINUE

Captain Kirk reacts to finding himself aboard the player's ship. Screenshot from *Star Trek Timelines,* developed and published by Disruptor Beam, Inc. and protected by United States and international copyright law. *Star Trek Timelines* © 2017 Disruptor Beam, Inc. STAR TREK™ & © 2017 CBS Studios Inc. © 2017 Paramount Pictures Corp. STAR TREK and related marks and logos are trademarks of CBS Studios Inc. All Rights Reserved.

It is important to note that both Kirk and Burnham react realistically to their situation, acknowledging it as strange and unexpected, as opposed to passively accepting that the player is now in control of them. This not only supports their characterization as established in their respective shows, but also shows the player that the developers take the integrity of the license seriously, and would never violate it simply to make things easier on themselves.

In *Star Trek*, Starfleet crews travel the Milky Way galaxy, which is divided into four quadrants, each populated with countless worlds and species. Actually building out countless worlds and species in-game can be challenging, if not impossible. Rather than overextend themselves, the *Star Trek Timelines* developers chose to flesh out only the Alpha Quadrant, the home of Starfleet and the United Federation of Planets. But the true size of the Milky Way isn't contradicted; rather, it is implied through the in-game galaxy map.

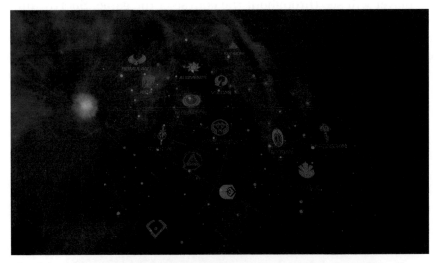

The Alpha Quadrant in *Star Trek Timelines*, and beyond. Screenshot from *Star Trek Timelines*, developed and published by Disruptor Beam, Inc. and protected by United States and international copyright law. *Star Trek Timelines* © 2017 Disruptor Beam, Inc. STAR TREK™ & © 2017 CBS Studios Inc. © 2017 Paramount Pictures Corp. STAR TREK and related marks and logos are trademarks of CBS Studios Inc. All Rights Reserved.

Only points of interest within the Alpha Quadrant may be visitable, but the empty quadrants surrounding reassure players that the writers did their homework and that additional content in other quadrants will be added to the game in the future.

In *Star Trek Timelines,* even features as far removed from narrative as the in-game store are imbued with license-appropriate flavor.

The player-facing name for the store is the "Time Portal," and when the player purchases items, they are shown emerging from the Guardian of Forever, an iconic alien object seen in the original *Star Trek* series, which once transported Captain Kirk and his crew to 1930s Earth and back again. When the Guardian of Forever has a valuable item to present, an audio clip from the episode itself is heard, the Guardian intoning, "BEHOLD!"

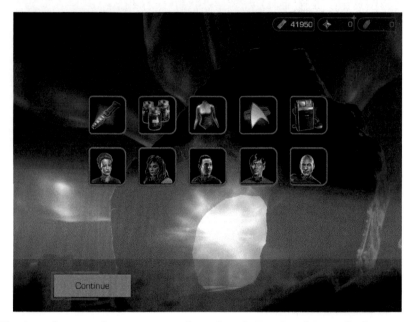

The player obtains supplies, equipment, and crew from the Time Portal. Screenshot from *Star Trek Timelines*, developed and published by Disruptor Beam, Inc. and protected by United States and international copyright law. *Star Trek Timelines* © 2017 Disruptor Beam, Inc. STAR TREK™ & © 2017 CBS Studios Inc. © 2017 Paramount Pictures Corp. STAR TREK and related marks and logos are trademarks of CBS Studios Inc. All Rights Reserved.

Additional features that do not lend themselves easily to narrative justification are also given appropriate context; "The Gauntlet," a PvP head-to-head crew battling system, is presented as both a training exercise for the player and entertainment for Q, a mercurial god-like being who first alerted the player to the presence of the temporal anomalies and enlisted him to help in sorting them out.

While *Star Trek* asks both its characters and its audience to ponder many deep questions, it also depicts a naval-based crew aboard a starship that must frequently enter dangerous space in order to complete its missions. Thus, any *Star Trek* game heavy on narrative introspection and light on action would not be true to the license, and *Star Trek*

Timelines ensures that the majority of its story is delivered in a way that requires the player to be actively engaged. Away team missions ask the player to first select three crew members with the relevant skills, and then break the mission down into stages, asking the player at each stage which action he wants to take, and with which crew member.

Will the player use diplomacy, medical knowledge, or engineering savvy to overcome Lore? Screenshot from *Star Trek Timelines*, developed and published by Disruptor Beam, Inc. and protected by United States and international copyright law. *Star Trek Timelines* © 2017 Disruptor Beam, Inc. STAR TREK™ & © 2017 CBS Studios Inc. © 2017 Paramount Pictures Corp. STAR TREK and related marks and logos are trademarks of CBS Studios Inc. All Rights Reserved.

Away team missions can be completed in a matter of minutes, and multiple missions may be required to complete an "episode" worth of content. This content organization method is well suited to the mobile platform, allowing players to feel as though they have accomplished something major in each play session. Though *Star Trek* itself is an enormous franchise spanning several decades and counting, with iterations on both television and the silver screen, *Star Trek Timelines* successfully combines and condenses them all into an engaging mobile experience.

Case Study #3: *The Walking Dead: March to War* (2017)

Robert Kirkman's *The Walking Dead* comics invite readers into a world where the afterlife is real—and it involves rotting flesh and feeding on the blood and sinew of your still-living friends and relatives. But in this brutal world, it is not the dead who should be feared most, and main character Rick Grimes's struggles to survive and keep hope alive in the face of this devastation have kept readers hooked for over 150 issues and counting. Disruptor Beam's *The Walking Dead: March to War* allows players to enter that war themselves, establishing their own community and fighting to protect it against the scavengers, marauders, and otherwise lost people of the world. Along the way, players may befriend Rick Grimes—or his brutal, grinning adversary, Negan—and decide for themselves whether there is any room in this new world for morality or hope.

The Walking Dead: March to War opens with a scripted experience that immediately presents several core elements of *The Walking Dead* license to the prospective player. A post-apocalyptic wasteland? Check. Reanimated corpses shambling toward the living? Check. Hilltop, an iconic canonical location, visually recognizable to fans? Check. High-affinity characters Rick Grimes, Michonne, and Jesus? Check.

Hilltop Colony, as depicted in *The Walking Dead: March to War*. Screenshot from *The Walking Dead: March to War*, developed and published by Disruptor Beam, Inc. and protected by United States and international copyright law. *The Walking Dead* Copyright© 2017 Robert Kirkman, LLC. All Rights Reserved.

Although *The Walking Dead: March to War* licenses the comics, not the AMC television series, the choice to feature only locations and characters that also appear on the television series (and more or less visually resemble their comic book counterparts) in the game's first moments was a deliberate one. This removes the barrier to entry for fans of the television series who may not be familiar with the comics, allowing them to feel as welcome in the game as fans of the comics.

Though the action of *The Walking Dead* comics begins in Kentucky, it quickly moves to Georgia, and then from there to Washington, DC, where Rick Grimes eventually assumes control of the permanent community known as the Alexandria Safe-Zone. There, he runs afoul of Negan, leader of a local group known as the Saviors, and it is their conflict of leadership that sets off the titular war in *The Walking Dead: March to War*. While it might have been easier to set the game in another area of the United States, so as to avoid disrupting canonical events, the game's writers chose instead to set the game where the action is, in the heart of DC itself. Canonical landmarks, such as the Washington Monument, can be seen and visited by the player's survivors, and it is among these ruins that the player sets up his own community.

The White House, abandoned to the dead. Screenshot from *The Walking Dead: March to War*, developed and published by Disruptor Beam, Inc. and protected by United States and international copyright law. *The Walking Dead* Copyright © 2017 Robert Kirkman, LLC. All Rights Reserved.

In *The Walking Dead* comics, there are a number of groups that have settled in the DC area, but *The Walking Dead: March to War* imagines hundreds, even thousands of player-created groups joining them. In order to resolve this conflict with canon, the writers chose to draw a line in the sand. The events of the comics up through the volume labeled *March to War* are assumed to have occurred, and it is at this point in the comics that *The Walking Dead: March to War* begins. From there, the storyline of the game can be considered an alternate universe in which a horde of walkers moves in to surround the DC area, forcing hundreds, even thousands, of groups into an area where there were fewer previously. *The Walking Dead: March to War* asks the player to imagine how this influx of new allies (or enemies) might affect the war between Rick and Negan, and how the players themselves would fit in. This narrative design allows the game's writers the flexibility to create new content while still honoring the major events that have shaped the characters' worldviews and personalities.

As a mobile war game, *The Walking Dead: March to War's* content is largely player-generated, borne from interaction with the in-game map. Players decide what to scavenge, where to defend, and whom to attack, establishing their own alliances, rivalries, and rules of engagement. This and many other in-game features are in keeping with the war game genre, but *The Walking Dead: March to War* imbues each feature with licensed flavor. Dilemmas, for example, is at its heart a common reengagement feature found in many mobile war games: a problem, question, or simply a piece of information is presented to the player at regular intervals, and the player acknowledges or responds and receives a reward. In *The Walking Dead: March to War*, however, this feature is adapted in a way that best fits the grim world of the license. Characters present moral, often life-or-death Dilemmas that directly affect the survivors living in the player's community, forcing the player to make difficult decisions in which there is usually no true right or wrong answer.

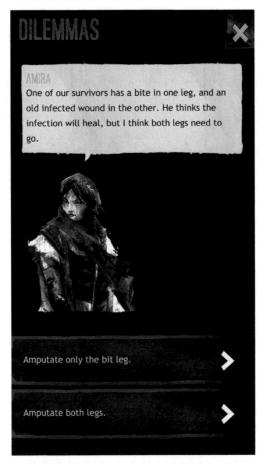

The player is presented with a Dilemma. Screenshot from *The Walking Dead: March to War*, developed and published by Disruptor Beam, Inc. and protected by United States and international copyright law. *The Walking Dead* Copyright © 2017 Robert Kirkman, LLC. All Rights Reserved.

Though the game's scope did not allow for branching storylines, *The Walking Dead: March to War* allows player choice by virtue of which content he chooses to acquire and complete. All canonical characters serve as optional Council members to the player, meaning that if the player pursues and unlocks them, they can lead his survivors on missions. Each Council member comes with an attached Council Story, a series of objectives for the player that allow him to build a deeper relationship with that Council member. If the player likes Negan's brutal ways, he can acquire Negan. If he finds Negan repulsive, he can choose not to pursue acquiring Negan at all. The player may find success in the game with any Council member; he is not required to unlock a specific one or all in order to win. In this way, *The Walking Dead:*

March to War provides the player with a feeling of agency over the narrative, without the added cost of a full-fledged branching storyline.

Finally, like other Disruptor Beam titles, *The Walking Dead: March to War* ensures that the license is reflected in all aspects of the game, not just story. Rick Grimes's fellow survivors are family to him; all of them have their own backstories, personalities, and memorable moments, which give the choices they make greater meaning, as well as affecting deeper sorrow upon their deaths. *The Walking Dead: March to War* seeks to give the player's survivors the same by giving them names, faces, unique facts, and circumstances in which the player encounters them. After reviewing all this information, the player may choose to recruit them into his community, or trade for supplies and allow them to go on their way.

The player weighs whether to recruit Kayla Knight into his community. Screenshot from *The Walking Dead: March to War*, developed and published by Disruptor Beam, Inc. and protected by United States and international copyright law. *The Walking Dead* Copyright © 2017 Robert Kirkman, LLC. All Rights Reserved.

These elements do not affect gameplay with a survivor in any way; her stats and talents are the only literal game changers. But giving each survivor this additional level of personalization imbues them with life and turns what could have been a straightforward mathematical equation into a roleplaying moment for the player, further immersing him in the world of *The Walking Dead*. Though the well-established mobile war game genre offered the developers many easy answers, they instead chose to go the extra mile with *The Walking Dead: March to War*, creating a rich experience that expands both the genre and the license to a whole new audience.

conclusion

Licenses are becoming more and more accessible, even to the independent developer, but making a good licensed game is rare. Making a good licensed *mobile* game is arguably even rarer. Writers must balance the licensor's needs and requirements against the developer's needs and requirements, all while keeping in mind the unique challenges of the mobile platform. Success starts with a good relationship with the licensor and deep familiarization with the license itself. Success is secured by establishing the license quickly, casting the audience net wide, ensuring the license is reflected in every aspect of the game, finding the narrative design that best fits both the license and the platform, and finally maintaining a high level of ambition throughout development. Licensed mobile games should not be viewed by developers or players as a cheap knock-off of a more expansive console or PC game, but rather the McDonald's toy-sized version. Equally recognizable, equally exciting—just in a smaller package!

as you prepare to write, ask yourself the following

What is the licensor's understanding of this license, and does it match mine?
- What are the core elements of this license?
- What has/hasn't worked best for this license?
- Are there any specific restrictions or sacred cows within this license?

- Will this game be considered canon?
- What FCC/MPAA rating has/would this license earn(ed)? What ESRB rating (hypothetical or otherwise) is desired for the game? If the two conflict, how can they be reconciled?
- How far and in what directions can you expand the existing canon of the license?
- What are the expectations in regards to an approvals process or a content creation pipeline?

Do I understand why this license is beloved and has so many fans? Have I become a fan myself?

as you revise, ask yourself the following

- Is the license identifiable and established within the player's first few seconds in the game?
- Is the player immersed in the license in every aspect of the game?
- Does the narrative design of the game fit the pace and style of both the license AND the mobile platform?
- Have I targeted casual fans before superfans? Will my game attract as many, if not more, casual fans as superfans?
- Despite being on a mobile platform, does my game rival the experience of playing a console or PC licensed game?

references and recommended reading

Batman: Arkham. Kentish Town, UK: Rocksteady Studios, 2009. Videogame.

Daglow, Don L. *Building Big Licensed Games with Big Teams.* Accessed September 8, 2017. http://twvideo01.ubm-us.net/o1 /vault/gdc04/slides/building_big_licensed.pdf

Despain, Wendy, ed. *Writing for Video Game Genres: From FPS to RPG.* 1st ed. Wellesley, MA: A K Peters, 2008.

Dornbush, Jonathan. "DICE 2017: Marvel Games to Tell Original Stories, Not Held to Canon" last modified February, 23 2017. http://www.ign.com/articles/2017/02/24/dice-2017-marvel -games-to-tell-original-stories-not-held-to-canon

Game of Thrones Ascent. Framingham, MA: Disruptor Beam, 2013. Videogame.

Goldberg, Lee, ed. *Tied In: The Business, History and Craft of Media Tie-In Writing*. Calabasas, CA: The International Association of Media Tie-In Writers, 2010.

Kim Kardashian: Hollywood. San Francisco: Glu Mobile, 2014. Videogame.

Klepek, Patrick. "How to Make the Best of Working on Licensed Video Games," last modified February 16, 2017. https://waypoint.vice .com/en_us/article/3djq7k/how-to-make-the-best-of-working -on-licensed-video-games

Marvel: Contest of Champions. San Francisco: Kabam, 2014. Videogame.

Peterson, Steve. "Why Licensed Games Are Finally Hot," last modified November 3, 2014. http://www.gamesindustry.biz/articles/2014 -11-03-why-licensed-games-are-finally-hot

Pink Zapper Helmet. "The Obvious (and Not so Obvious) Problem with Licensed Games," last modified June 22, 2014. http:// tay.kinja.com/the-obvious-and-not-so-obvious-problem-with -licensed-1587604957

Silberberger, Dan. "How to License IP for Mobile Games, Part 1," last modified September 30, 2014. https://www.linkedin.com /pulse/20140930152714-772702-how-to-license-ip-for-mobile -games-part-1

The Simpsons: Tapped Out. Los Angeles, CA: Electronic Arts, 2012. Videogame.

South Park: The Fractured but Whole. Rennes, FR: Ubisoft, 2017. Videogame.

South Park: The Stick of Truth. Rennes, FR: Ubisoft, 2014. Videogame.

Star Trek Timelines. Framingham, MA: Disruptor Beam, 2016. Videogame.

The Walking Dead. San Rafael, CA: Telltale Games, 2012. Videogame.

The Walking Dead: March to War. Framingham, MA: Disruptor Beam, 2017. Videogame.

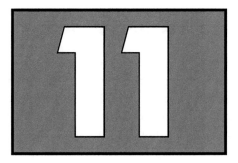

buy gems to woo your lover
free-to-play narratives

Eddy Webb

contents

"Free to play." How alluring those three words seem. A world of entertainment is just a tap away, and all for free! But that's not entirely true. Companies have other ways of coaxing money out of dedicated mobile players. The strategies even seem to form their own arcane language. "Freemium." "Microtransactions." "Integrated advertisements." Sometimes free-to-play games seem more focused on marketing metrics and monetization techniques than narrative design. But don't let dense buzzwords and unusual financial strategies fool you: free-to-play designs have plenty of opportunities to tell an engaging story. It's just a matter of understanding how to craft your narrative accordingly.

gates and keys: free-to-play design

But first, let's digress for a moment to talk about free-to-play game design. These games are free to download and install and, at first, they offer a compelling and frictionless experience for a couple of hours. After a certain point, however, elements of the game hamper or restrict further progress. The player is encouraged to spend money on in-game items or currency that reduce time spent waiting, make a task easier, or provide the resources needed to continue playing the game.

These *microtransactions* are where the free-to-play model becomes financially successful. While there are a wide variety of possible microtransaction models ranging from adding new characters to cosmetic upgrades, we're going to focus on those that allow players to progress in the game. Whenever an in-game event blocks a player's progress (a timer, a difficult puzzle, a missing resource), we'll call that a *gate*. Similarly, a purchase made to overcome that event (in-game currency, a buff, a resource generator) will be called a *key*. A key unlocks a gate.

Ads: Gate or Key?

As an aside, many free-to-play games serve up advertisements as a way of generating income. From a design perspective, watching advertisements can be either a gate or a key. If watching the ad is optional, allowing the player the choice to watch in exchange for a resource, then ads becomes another avenue of microtransaction—essentially, the company purchasing ad space is buying a key on behalf of the player. However, if the ad is mandatory, it becomes a gate of its own, and the key to unlock it is spending time with the ad. Given that the content of the ads is usually out of the control of the hosting game, it's difficult to integrate them into narrative design (although integrating the *concept* of watching ads isn't).

A successful free-to-play game makes getting past the gate more attractive than not playing the game. Some games make the gate impossible to pass without the needed key—DLC content packs are a good example. These *hard gates* need something particularly compelling on the other side to get the player to buy the needed key, but at least the sales pitch is straightforward: cough up some money if you want to see more of the game.

But in many cases, what the player is buying is ease of access. The gate itself is time or difficulty, and given enough patience or skill, a player could theoretically overcome it. These *soft gates* are potentially permeable without purchasing access, but keys make bypassing the gate easier. The "secret sauce" of soft gate design is that the player needs to keep engaging with the game to overcome the gate. As such, there are more opportunities to encourage the purchase of a key—a steady stream of upselling that can generate more microtransactions.

Moving back to narrative design, the role of story in free-to-play design can work in two ways. Story can help the player understand why the gate is there, and why buying a key would be desirable. It can also be used as an incentive, encouraging the player to purchase a key to get to the next part of the story. Many times, the narrative design will offer a bit of both but, in general, one will be considered the key design goal of the narrative. Let's call these *story-as-context* and *story-as-reward*.

story-as-context

In story-as-context, the narrative gives a framework for the gates. How and why the player struggles in the game becomes important, and an engaging and entertaining story context encourages the player to continue investing time, energy, and (hopefully) money. A good example of story-as-context is the visual novel genre, with games like the *Ace Attorney* series—the mechanics of play in the courtroom scenes of *Ace Attorney* games are impossible to decouple from the story without making the gameplay meaningless.

When your project has context as the narrative goal, always remember that each moment needs to tie into the story, even if it's in a small way. It's necessary to let the game elements come through to provide the substance of the gate, but the player should never feel like the story has stopped and the "game part" has taken over. Gameplay should feel like it's a part of the story, or else the context is lost. When crafting the play experience, always ask yourself, "How does this work into the story?"

Sometimes the best story context isn't provided in words. Art assets, font choice, music, and sound effects can provide and enhance the story frame. As the narrative designer, you'll need to work with other departments and come to agreements on how each piece of the design works with and enhances the story. This is true on many projects, but particularly when the story provides the context for all gameplay. In story-as-context, *everything* drives the story, which then drives the microtransaction model, so the better the story, the more money the game will make.

However, all-inclusive narrative requires buy-in at the earliest stages of design. In principle, the whole team needs to be on board with such a direction, and someone (ideally a lead narrative designer or writer) makes sure that the story is being served appropriately every step of the way. In practice, it can be difficult to keep such focus, particularly if the team is large or if the design becomes financially unfeasible. This can lead to either the game mechanics falling away (leaving microtransactions as a key to unlock a simple "buy the next chapter" gate), or story taking a back seat to the mechanics (often pushing it more to a story-as-reward model).

Example: *Tunnels & Trolls Adventures* (2017)

Back in the 1970s and early 1980s, when tabletop roleplaying games were still emerging as an art form, *Tunnels & Trolls* (1975) was the second-ever fantasy RPG system to be commercially produced. However, tabletop roleplaying games require a group of players to be in the same physical area, like most board and card games. The company that produced *Tunnels & Trolls*, Flying Buffalo Inc., recognized that players might have trouble getting a group of players together, or otherwise want to play the game by themselves. As such, they produced a series of successful solo adventures to address that need.

In 2017, a company called MetaArcade acquired the *Tunnels & Trolls* license and designed the *Tunnels & Trolls* app containing digital versions of those solo adventures. MetaArcade asked me to help with the translation of these classic modules from pencil-and-dice gaming to mobile. Because I sensed this would be a design of story-as-context, some of the earliest questions I asked were, "How do microtransactions work, and how does it work to drive the story?"

The core microtransaction revolves around access to adventures. A Heart allows the player to play an adventure once, until the character fails, succeeds, or quits—the analogy given to me was putting a quarter into a classic video arcade machine.

A Gem allows the player to play through an adventure as many times as they want, which is more like buying the game and taking it home to play. Hearts and Gems can be purchased via microtransaction, and Hearts can also be acquired by watching ads.

This barrier to entry is a classic hard gate: the player needs a key (a Heart or a Gem) to gain access. Viewing ads offers another method of generating keys besides real-world money, but no amount of waiting or skill will allow a player to pass that gate. Without a key, they can't play, period. However, the gate itself is not framed within the story—we haven't even gotten to the story yet! While this is a good example of a hard gate and key, it's not embedded in the narrative design. So, let's dig a little deeper.

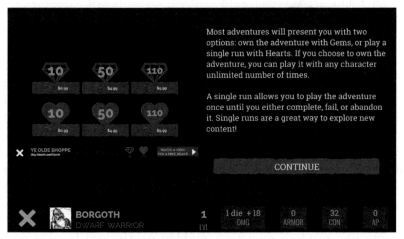

Example 1: Illustration of the microtransaction model. Screenshot from *Tunnels & Trolls Adventures*. Developed/published by MetaArcade and is protected by United States and international copyright law. © MetaArcade

Once you have access to the adventure, you create or choose a character with RPG stats, which acts as an avatar in an interactive text adventure. Images and sound effects are added to promote the story context, but the focus is on the text itself. The art and sound aren't required to understand the unfolding story—many mobile users play games with the sound turned off, for example—but they illustrate how important it is to the design team that the story is the focus at every step.

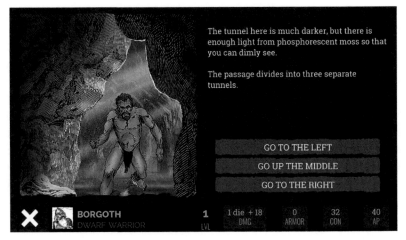

The tunnel here is much darker, but there is enough light from phosphorescent moss so that you can dimly see.

The passage divides into three separate tunnels.

GO TO THE LEFT

GO UP THE MIDDLE

GO TO THE RIGHT

BORGOTH
DWARF WARRIOR

1
LVL

1 die + 18
DMG

0
ARMOR

32
CON

40
AP

Example 2: While art is important, equal focus is on the text and the decisions presented to the player. Screenshot from *Tunnels & Trolls Adventures*. Developed/published by MetaArcade and is protected by United States and international copyright law. © MetaArcade

Furthermore, *Tunnels & Trolls Adventures* is specifically replicating a tabletop gaming experience. Instead of having numbers generated in the background, the game has virtual dice that roll, bounce, and scatter across the screen at key moments, like combat and skill tests. Each screen pushes the feeling that you're at a table playing a gripping and adventurous fantasy story game.

While the inclusion of dice can look like an intrusion of "game" into the "story" context, that isn't the case here. By including virtual dice, a *style* of storytelling—that of old-school fantasy gaming—is preserved. With that genre visually established and reinforced, narrative concepts like random monsters, sudden death, and bizarre coincidence can be more easily included. If the game were focused purely on story, then it would be more difficult for the player to swallow such a level of randomness in the narrative. But because these things are common in tabletop roleplaying games and solo gamebooks, they're seen as more acceptable. In this way, the game mechanic of "generate random numbers to compare to a character statistic" is pitched to enhance and preserve narrative integrity.

Dice Frame Randomness

But why use dice at all? Because most people understand that physical dice are, by design, random. By showing dice, readers accept that randomness is appropriate to the narrative—otherwise, without providing feedback, the player has no way of knowing that the game isn't just arbitrarily causing them to succeed, fail, or die. Even though in both cases the computer is generating numbers, people accept that *dice* are random, and therefore tolerate it more. Paradoxically, the player can feel more in control of the narrative if random results are shown rather than hidden.

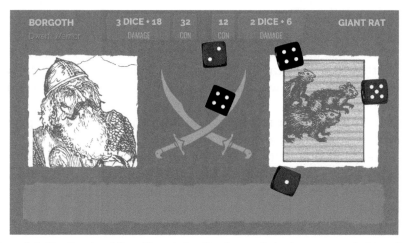

Example 3: Showing virtual dice adds to, rather than detracts from, the story context. Screenshot from *Tunnels & Trolls Adventures*. Developed/published by MetaArcade and is protected by United States and international copyright law. © MetaArcade

The positioning of random elements front and center helps the narrative design in another aspect. Many of these adventures are *hard*, and intentionally so. Players can keep any equipment and experience their characters acquire during the adventure, even if they fail and survive (they don't keep the equipment if they die, but they still keep the experience earned). This makes the character more likely to succeed on the next playthrough. Since the dice are realized on the screen, players can attribute failure to a bad dice roll, rather than game design capriciousness. Maybe *this* time the player can roll well to defeat the giant rats. Maybe *this* time the player can make a decision more in line with how her character is evolving mechanically. Maybe *this* time the player can move the story along just a little further.

In this way, the difficulty and the randomness of the game both act as soft gates. As mentioned earlier, this could be a good place to introduce microtransactions for keys to overcome these gates, and many games do exactly that. Interestingly, *Tunnels & Trolls Adventures* doesn't, at least not currently. In a way, the difficulty and randomness are not obstacles to overcome, but rather are part and parcel of the old-school tabletop experience they're emulating. These are features, not bugs, and that's what their intended audience wants. And, should they desire, MetaArcade might introduce those microtransactions later for players who aren't as enamored with that particular experience.

Such difficulty encourages replayability, which encourages players to consider the purchase of more Hearts or Gems to try again. While these soft gates don't directly have corresponding keys, they do push players back to the main microtransaction model. The story is not a reward for bypassing the gates, but a means (and an experience) unto itself.

story-as-reward

More commonly, free-to-play games will frame the narrative as something to be acquired, rather than an inherent part of the overall experience. The cadence of gameplay is more divided: you play the game for a while, and after you pass the gate, a new piece of the story is offered as a prize. This is story-as-reward, and it can be seen in puzzle games, first-person shooters, or even RPGs—franchises such as *Uncharted* and *Mass Effect* make effective use of this structure.

In many cases, the narrative in story-as-reward could be stripped out of the project with little to no impact on the overall mechanics of the game. It's largely or entirely decoupled from the core game design, which means that the narrative may be produced in isolation, in parallel, or even after the basic design of the project is established.

However, how much the player values the story depends on the experience that delivers it. So, while the initial narrative design isn't as interdependent as it is in story-as-context, it's still important. The more the narrative is embedded into the context of the "game" portion of the experience, the more the "narrative" portion will be appreciated. A lot of what we covered previously applies here as well: working with art, animation, audio design, and other disciplines to embed the narrative in every aspect of the game makes the award of new story elements that much more rewarding.

Furthermore, players need to be invested in the story in the beginning. The first elements of the story need to be freely or easily available, to get the player interested or emotionally invested. Think of it like reading the first chapter or two of a novel in a bookstore or as a preview online; if the reader gets hooked, they're more likely to pay to find out what happens next. The same can happen with free-to-play narratives as well.

Finally, because players aren't constantly immersed in the narrative, it's possible for long periods of time to pass before the player gets to the next beat. As such, the player should never feel lost in the story. Easy-to-access recaps and summaries help keep the player up to date, but offering a steady stream of low-impact world details like diary entries or background information can remind the player what's exciting about your narrative and encourage them to push through the next gate.

Example: *Futurama: Game of Drones* (2015)

Futurama (1999) is a cartoon created by Matt Groening, of *The Simpsons* fame. While it has been cancelled and restarted a few times over the years, it has remained a popular and enduring franchise. Wooga acquired the rights to produce a *Futurama* mobile game, entitled *Futurama: Game of Drones*.

Early on, a team of writers (including the show's lead writer, Patric Verrone) consulted on the game's design. Wooga was very keen to have the story of *Futurama* as a central element of *Game of Drones*. I was brought on to help with scriptwriting and other narrative tasks after the initial narrative design was done, but I got a good sense of why the narrative was designed the way it was.

When a player starts *Game of Drones,* they are immediately shown a comic featuring the characters of the show. Right away, the characters and the story are positioned as central to the game experience, and players have a chance to learn about the world of *Futurama* and laugh at the predicaments these characters are put into.

Example 4: The game starts with story, teaching the player both the narrative framework of the game and showing them the potential narrative "prize" of additional comics. Screenshot from *Futurama: Game of Drones.* Developed/published by Wooga and is protected by United States and international copyright law. © Wooga

This first comic not only teaches the player what the narrative framework of the game will be, but also shows them the narrative "prize" that is possible: additional full-screen comics that are individually entertaining and progress the ongoing story. (Later, the player learns there are also modals of characters simply talking to each other—these are more frequent and less plot relevant, but often contain interesting character moments and entertaining one-liners in the spirit of the original show.)

After the opening comic and a quick tutorial, the game shows one of hundreds of levels. Each level is a drone-matching puzzle that the player must solve. This drone-matching is explained within the game's narrative, but the act of solving the puzzle does not progress the story. Instead, learning more about the story of *Game of Drones* is what drives the player on, encouraging them to solve the puzzles.

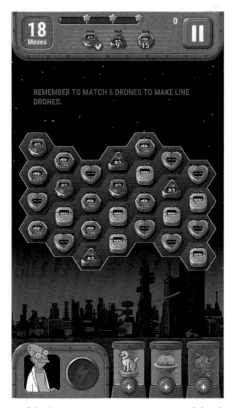

Example 5: While elements of the Futurama series are present in each level, such as the theme song, characters, and art assets, the levels themselves do not contribute to or progress the ongoing narrative. Screenshot from *Futurama: Game of Drones*. Developed/published by Wooga and is protected by United States and international copyright law. © Wooga

Over time, puzzles become more difficult. Drones on the board are also semirandomized, so a particular "shuffle" of drones might make a level hard, but a replay may be easier. Failing to complete a puzzle causes the player to lose a life, which comes back over time. Once players are out of lives, they cannot attempt any more puzzles. Both the difficulty and economy of lives present soft gates to a player's progress within the narrative.

Like many match-four games of its ilk, *Game of Drones* offers plenty of opportunities to generate Bucks (the game's currency), which can be spent to purchase more lives, as well as items that help with particularly tricky puzzles. These keys allow the player to overcome tricky soft gates, but the player can apply patience and skill to puzzles as well to proceed.

As the game progresses, it is likely that the time between story plot elements will get longer and longer. *Game of Drones* addresses this in a couple of interesting ways. The first is a library that archives previously unlocked comics so that players reread them at their leisure, allowing them to remind themselves of past plot points. Furthermore, the designers created a fake social media site inside the game called "Twitcher." This allows players to get small drips of content (not plot related), so there is always something novel whenever they log back into the game. This is important, as it keeps player enthusiasm and interest high, and pushes them to consider microtransactions to see more of the story.

Example 6: Low-impact narrative, such as Twitcher, allows *Game of Drones* to keep players excited about the story, encouraging them to push through soft gates—ideally through microtransactions. Screenshot from *Futurama: Game of Drones.* Developed/published by Wooga and is protected by United States and international copyright law. © Wooga

tips on crafting free-to-play narrative

Work with microtransactions, not against them: Free-to-play projects can't ignore the vital role that microtransactions have in the game's design. Whenever possible, find ways to integrate the microtransaction into the experience, if not the narrative. In humorous games, poking a little fun at the microtransaction model can help make it feel less intrusive—*Game of Drones* does this by using the Robot Devil as the spokesperson (spokesrobot?) for viewing ads in exchange for in-game currency. *Tunnels & Trolls Adventures*, on the other hand, leans into its old-school paper-and-dice roleplaying experience. It gives the player beautiful, artistic covers for each of its adventures and a small teaser of what's inside, to replicate a bookshelf of books with back-cover text. Both approaches play to the narrative experience's strengths, rather than making the microtransaction more of an annoyance.

Brevity is not simplicity: As with any mobile narrative, brevity is important in free-to-play stories. Screen real estate is at a premium, so every word and art asset counts. However, don't confuse "brevity" with "simplicity." How complex and intricate a story you design isn't constrained by the number of characters you can write at a time. *Game of Drones*, for example, is a complex story of revenge, exploration, and incompetence, spanning dozens of locations and featuring a large cast of characters. However, each beat of the story is carefully pared down to read and look exciting on a mobile device.

Never assume plot retention: When designing in story-as-reward, it might be minutes, hours, days, or even weeks for the player between plot points. Even when creating a story-as-context project, though, the player might be constantly engaged with the story, but they still might skim over a section or accidentally click through a screen of vital lore. Whenever possible, write pieces of content in ways that don't rely on the player having to remember other content. If player memory of an event is important, however, give a way for the player to easily refresh their memory. *Game of Drones* addresses this by providing an archive of plot-important comics. *Tunnels & Trolls Adventures* assumes the player is going through an adventure all at once, but replaying the adventure gives the players a chance to catch details they missed the first time.

Novelty is important: When you're trying to get players to come back to your game as often as possible, your story can't go stale. As soon as the player feels like they're not getting anything interesting from the narrative, they'll skip microtransactions, or even uninstall the game to play something else. Whenever possible, introduce plot twists, new characters, an unfamiliar perspective, or new locations. *Tunnels & Trolls Adventures* has completely different adventures for players to choose from, and the randomness of specific events inside the adventures means that multiple playthroughs aren't identical. *Game of Drones* changes the location and central character every 25 levels or so, so things feel fresh.

conclusion and checklist questions

Narrative in a free-to-play game is as important as your team wants it to be. Whether you're using narrative as context for the entire experience or as a juicy reward after difficult levels, the more the entire team is invested in the narrative, the more the story will work to serve that goal. Having a strong narrative design lead can certainly help to assure that every aspect of the game's design is working with and reinforcing the narrative, but a team that's completely behind the concept of the game's narrative is worth its weight in gold.

Whenever the impact of the narrative seems to be drifting, or if there's a problem in marrying the narrative to one of the game's mechanics, asking these questions of the team can help bring things back into focus:

What is the story doing here? It's always important to confirm that the story is moving along as needed every step of the way, and that changes over time haven't diluted or changed the narrative intent. However, too much emphasis on the story can get in the way of the game experience. A microtransaction screen might be heavily embedded in the story's lore, but the actual experience of giving the game money might be clunky and difficult as a result. Sometimes, the best answer is to have the story step aside.

How does this moment serve the story? If there's an element of the design that's not serving the story, it's natural to call it into question. Sometimes you can't simply excise that aspect of the design, but perhaps there's a way to frame or subvert the design so that it does help the narrative, rather than work against it.

Will the player be excited by this? More of a concern for story-as-reward, but you should look to every narrative moment with an eye toward player engagement. If the player simply pushed a button to get more story, you wouldn't have to worry as much as if the player worked for hours and spent a lot of money to get there. However, even "easy" moments should have momentum to keep player interest. If there's not much happening, reframe it in a more exciting and interesting way. Be particularly wary of "infodumps"* and other lengthy-but-informative moments in your story.

Can this be pared down? Are you trying to communicate too much in a small moment? There are only so many characters you can put on a mobile screen, and only so much detail to be easily discerned from an art piece. If there's a lot to cover, consider spreading the information across several screens or, even better, carefully doled out across separate gameplay moments with gates in between.

Is this moment necessary? One of the hardest moments for a writer is the recognition that a favorite line or bit of dialogue is clever, entertaining, and utterly unnecessary to the experience. If a narrative moment is causing problems for the design, sometimes it's best to simply scrap it and move on.

F2P tips

- Understand your microtransaction model.
  - Structure your narrative design around the model, instead of ignoring it or working against it.

---

* An "infodump" is a narrative device where a character explains the situation. In general, it's better to avoid them—particularly because of small mobile screens.

- Determine if your narrative's goal is to act as a context or as a reward.
    - If context, make sure every aspect of design works with the narrative.
    - If reward, keep the player intrigued about the narrative in the gaps between story beats.
- Find ways to frame your microtransactions that work with the narrative.
    - You want the player to keep playing, and microtransactions are a big part of that.
- Make sure each story beat is brief but significant.
    - However, don't confuse "brief" with "simple"—you can introduce complex narratives in brief beats.
- Design straightforward ways for players to review the narrative thus far.
    - Make sure they never feel lost in the story.
- Keep changing things up in your narrative as players progress.
    - As soon as the story feels like the same old thing, players will drop out.

index

Page numbers followed by f and t indicate figures and tables, respectively.